Arnold Palmer's Complete Book of Putting

Arnold Palmer's Complete Book of Putting

Arnold Palmer
and
Peter Dobereiner

Stanley Paul
London Melbourne Auckland Johannesburg

Stanley Paul & Co. Ltd

An imprint of Century Hutchinson Ltd

62–65 Chandos Place, London WC2N 4NW

Century Hutchinson (Australia) Pty Ltd
16–22 Church Street, Hawthorn, Melbourne, Victoria 3122

Century Hutchinson (NZ) Ltd
32–34 View Road, Glenfield, Auckland 10

Century Hutchinson (SA) Pty Ltd
PO Box 337, Bergvlei 2012, South Africa

First published in USA by Atheneum 1986
First published in Great Britain 1986

Printed and bound in Great Britain by Scotprint Ltd,
Musselburgh

ISBN 0 09 163910 7

To Our Future Golfers
Our Grandchildren
Emily, Katy, and Annie
and
Rebecca, Rachel, and Georgina

With Grateful Acknowledgments . . .

To the United States Golf Association and the Royal and Ancient Golf Club of St. Andrews for permission to reproduce Rules 16 and 17

To George O'Grady, Tournament Director of the European PGA Tour, for technical assistance with the Rules

To Cassell and Company for permission to reproduce extracts from *Bobby Jones on Golf*

To Mrs. Elspeth Crawley for permission to reproduce an article by the late Leonard Crawley

To *Country Life* for permission to reproduce extracts from *Bobby Locke on Golf*

To Methuen and Company for permission to reproduce extracts by Walter Travis from *Great Golfers in the Making*

To Hodder and Stoughton, Ltd., for permission to reproduce extracts by John Low from *Concerning Golf*

To the Longman Group for permission to reproduce extracts by A. J. Balfour from The Badminton Library: *Golf*

CONTENTS

INTRODUCTION

I am a golfer and not much of a hand at the writing game. Peter Dobereiner is a writer and, in spite of what he says when he has been at the red wine, he is no great shakes as a golfer. The theory behind collaborations like this one is that the book will represent the best of two talents. But do not get the idea that we sat down side by side and that I whispered pearls of wisdom into his ear and he transcribed them onto his typewriter in deathless prose. These partnerships cannot work like that.

For a start, nobody could ever get me to sit still for that long. For another thing, journalists are a funny breed. I have spent a lot of time among newspaper guys because I enjoy swapping stories and beers as much as any man. But writers do have curious methods of working. Just as golfers can hit only so many shots in a day, so writers can produce only so many words in a day. If they work for newspapers their daily ration of words has to be produced at high speed, against a deadline, and that furious burst of activity leaves them with nothing much to do for the rest of the day. That's why they prop up the bar. Sometimes they get so bored that they even stroll out on the golf course—I know because I've seen them out there from time to time. So, when it comes to writing books, they work at odd moments, scribbling away on long flights or late at night when honest citizens are tucked in bed. Thus there was no way that Dobereiner and I could play this thing like a duet, not even on long air trips, because most of the time when I am flying to, say, California, he is en route to cover the Spanish Open. Besides, when I fly I like to keep my mind on the job of flying the plane.

Of course, we did get together. At times it seemed that he asked me a lot of questions I couldn't decipher, and I gave him a load of answers he didn't understand—the old problem when a Pennsylvania boy tries to converse with an Englishman. But we have known each other for twenty-five years and have had many sessions together in different parts of the world. Goodness knows how many of my interviews he has had to sit through. The great champion Harry Vardon once said that he never knew how well he had played until he read Bernard Darwin's report in the next day's *Times,* and I guess that by now Dobereiner knows pretty well how I think and what my views are on the game of golf. And I touched up his text and put him back on track when he went off the rails too badly.

In his library Peter has thirty-three yards of golf books and he has read them all. He says he perpetrated thirty-one inches of the thirty-three yards himself, not counting this book. Including newspaper and magazine articles, he has written the equivalent of two whole bibles on the subject of golf and is now up to Nehemiah for the third time around. Even if he has never had

"This for the Open," he has talked about it with every champion since the prime of Ben Hogan during his lifelong study of the game. So we are not quite in the position of George Bernard Shaw when he was approached by a gorgeous actress with the proposition that they should make a baby because with her looks and his brain the child must be an outstanding human being. The gruff old Irish playwright pointed out the obvious danger, that the child might inherit his looks and her brain and would be a walking disaster. Personally, I think he turned down a pretty good offer, but that's neither here nor there. At least I can guarantee that this book does not consist of Dobereiner's ideas expressed in my words.

Nor is it 100 percent my ideas expressed in his words. For instance, I do not put my faith in plumb-bobbing for the line of a putt, preferring to rely on my eye and judgment and experience to read the break. But plumb-bobbing must have a place in a comprehensive book on putting and so you will find it fully discussed, .along with the advantages claimed for it by those who use the method, as well as with my reservations. We also examine the styles of successful putters who use techniques totally different from my own. Thus this is not a book on how to putt like Arnold Palmer—although there is plenty of that advice—but more a guide to golfers on how to discover methods that work for them individually. There is only one test of a putting method: *Does it work?* That is the bottom line, and so we have ranged widely over the entire subject. Putting is not an exact science so it is impossible to lay down firm rules. Mostly it is a matter of feel and mood and experience.

My purpose in this book has been to distill what I know about putting from fifty years in the game so that others may take a short-cut, avoiding the mistakes I made by trial and error and absorbing in one volume the proven conclusions I have reached. But I admit that there are other ways, other theories, and inevitably Dobereiner has put his personal slant on some of them. He is an opinionated writer, and leopards don't change their spots. But that's just fine by me, because I would never claim to have a monopoly on golfing wisdom, any more than I would accuse him of having a monopoly on dud ideas. We can coexist in one book, along with golfers who have demonstrated that they, too, knew a thing or two about putting.

All I ask is that if you come across a passage in the following pages that strikes you as utter nonsense, then blame Dobereiner. And when you read something that sparkles with the authentic gleam of a jewel of revelation, then give me the credit!

And may you one-putt every green.

Arnold Palmer
Latrobe, Pennsylvania, 1986

Arnold Palmer's Complete Book of Putting

A World of
Four and One-Quarter
Inches
in Diameter

GOLF. It is a science—the study of a lifetime in which you may exhaust yourself but never your subject.
—David Forgan

If we could go back through history to those fabulous days when Kublai Khan was the leading money-winner on the rape and pillage circuit, we could find men playing a game we would recognize as golf. That would be in Holland. It is possible that the same game was being played on the east coast of Scotland at that time. But it is impossible to award the glory, or the blame, for inventing golf to either Holland or Scotland because we simply do not have enough evidence either way.

What we do have is a mass of irrefutable evidence that golf, or *colf* as it was called, was played in Holland from at least the year 1297 onward. The first written record of Scottish golf, or *goff*, or *gowf*, does not occur until 160 years later—just a few decades before Christopher Columbus deliberately sailed off in the wrong direction in the belief that he was pioneering a shortcut to India and wound up discovering a new continent that came to be called America. That the Dutch game is well documented by city ordinances granting land for *colf* courses and court records detailing fines (often the forfeiture of their clothes) of golfers who caused damage or nuisance by playing inside the city walls is not proof that the Dutch invented golf. Literacy was rare in Scotland in those days, and there may well have been no call to commit to paper references to a pastime confined to a tiny minority.

The argument about who invented golf has been thoroughly obscured by Scottish historians whose patriotism was stronger than their scholarship. Professor Douglas Young, of St. Andrews University, claims baldly that "golf was invented soon after the foundation of St. Andrews University (1414)," without giving a shred of evidence for that statement and in defiance of the well-established fact that, by then, the game had been in existence for more than a hundred years. Another Scottish historian, Robert Browning, built up an impressive case against the Dutch connection by proving that *het kolven* bore no resemblance to golf, as well might be the case

since there never was such a game; it was a pure invention, a fictional pastime created from a mixture of ignorance, misinterpretation, and chauvinism.

What is certain is that during the period under discussion, there was a constant traffic between Holland and the Scottish east coast ports by fishermen, traders, and mercenary soldiers. The affinity between the coast of Fife and Holland was much closer than it was to Scotland's west coast, where golf did not take root until the eighteenth century. So, if a popular game developed either in St. Andrews or Haarlem, the news of this craze would have been transported across the North Sea within a matter of days. We also know that Dutch golf balls were imported into Scotland in vast numbers and that Scottish cleeks were exported to Holland. On the whole, then, the Dutch have the better case as inventors of golf, but the claim is by no means conclusive. Debate is ultimately futile—and what does it matter anyway?

By the time the officers of the Honourable Company of Edinburgh Golfers set down the earliest known written rules of golf the game had died out in Holland, and so those worthy Scots took as their model the code of the French game of *mail*. It is probable that golfers had managed without written rules for three hundred years because theirs was a wonderfully simple game, played more or less at random over the natural linksland. One feature, however, distinguished golf from other cross-country club-and-ball games, that being the putting of a ball into a hole.

The first recorded putt is illustrated in a Book of Hours (1500), but we can surmise that putting in the early days of golf bore little resemblance to the modern ritual on the green. For a start, there was no green, just a hole, which may well have been a rabbit scrape in those informal times. The first rules said that you had to tee up within a club's length of the hole, and you did this by picking a handful of sand out of the hole and making a conical mound on which to set your ball. We can imagine the state of the ground around the hole, as well as how the scooping of sand from the hole would quickly enlarge it. So putting then must have been more like chipping the ball into a bucket, as some of the old prints graphically show.

The earliest Dutch *colf* players used only one club, and the same is almost certainly true of the devotees of *goff*. Such a club would have to be lofted (equivalent to about a four-iron in the earliest known Dutch clubs) if it were to propel the *colf* balls of turned hardwood, and so putting in the sense that we understand it today would have been impossible. Gradually the rules were changed, requiring the player to tee his ball not nearer than two club's lengths of the hole (1776), not nearer than four club's lengths (1851), not nearer than six club's lengths (1859), and not nearer than eight club's lengths (1875). In the latter year the first mention occurs of a separate teeing ground, and sand boxes for building tees were introduced five years later. But the development that paved the way for formal putting greens was the invention of the mechanical mower in 1830. Hand-scything continued for many years thereafter, but in 1893 the evolution of the game was completed by the formal definition of the teeing ground and the codification of the hole at four and one-quarter inches in diameter.

It remains a mystery how the legislators settled on that precise size for the hole. There was no common measurement of four and one-quarter inches; the "hand" used in measuring the height of horses was four inches. The explanation may be humdrum, such as four and one-quarter being the standard internal dimension of drainpiping or drainage tiles and therefore a readily available source of material for making hole-cutters and liners. At all events, the four-and-one-quarter-inch hole has proved to be a diabolically enduring feature of golf. When the United States Golf Association (USGA) raised the minimum size of the golf ball to 1.68 inches in diameter, it was widely and passionately ar-

gued that the size of the hole should be increased pro rata.

In addition to the problems of holing out on ground that was also used for teeing up the ball, our forebears had to cope with another threat to their composure: the stymie. Golfers born since World War II will have had no experience of the stymie because it was finally abolished in 1951, thereby putting an end to the longest and most vituperative argument in the history of the game. Public opinion was evenly divided on the virtues or evils of the stymie, and the historian Horace Hutchinson recounts the reaction of one peppery colonel: "Sir, any man who wishes to abolish the stymie would willingly break any law in the land." The Royal and Ancient Golf Club of St. Andrews abolished the stymie in 1833, and we can judge the depth of feeling aroused by the change by the fact that it was restored by the club the following year.

The stymie rule simply said that if a player whose ball lay nearer the hole should play out of turn and putt out, the ball must be replaced immediately. The effect of this rule was that if your ball lay directly on the path of your opponent's putt, any sporting instincts on your part to get your ball out of his way must be rigorously stifled. The only exception was that if the two balls were within six inches of each other, the ball nearer the hole might be lifted, at the option of either player or opponent. In some quarters it was considered to be bad form to play deliberately for a stymie, although that convention was by no means universally endorsed and another school of thought held that laying a stymie on purpose was a perfectly legitimate stratagem and an integral part of the game.

Stymies played a decisive part in settling some crucial issues, including Bobby Jones's Grand Slam in 1930. In the fourth round of the British Amateur Championship against Cyril Tolley, Jones had to go to extra holes, and he wrote later: "I particularly regretted winning at the nineteenth hole by the aid of a stymie which was almost impossible to negotiate." Bobby

Fischer looked a certainty to go down by two and one against Jack McLean in the U.S. Amateur Championship of 1936 at Garden City when a fortuitous stymie at the thirty-fourth hole kept him in the match, which he won at the first extra hole.

But it was an incident in the English Close Amateur Championship of 1951 at Hunstanton which surely drove the last nail into the coffin of the stymie. In the final, G. P. Roberts and H. Bennett were all square as they came to the thirty-ninth green. Bennett, however, was hopelessly stymied, and so the title was clearly seen to have been decided by the sheer chance of one ball rolling to a stop stone dead on line of the other. Later that year the United States Golf Association and the Royal and Ancient Golf Club met for a rules conference and abolished the stymie once and for all.

A similar conference thirty years earlier had fixed the specifications of the golf ball at a minimum diameter of 1.62 inches (later raised unilaterally to 1.68 inches by the USGA) and a maximum weight of 1.62 ounces. At the same time the two ruling bodies announced that they would take whatever steps they thought necessary to limit the powers of the ball with regard to distance, should any ball of greater power be introduced. By this time (1920) the rubber-core ball was well established in the form that has endured in its basic construction to this day—elastic thread wound under tension over a central core and encased in a cover of gutta percha, later superseded by thermoplastic or rubber compounds. The standardization of the size and weight of golf balls had obvious repercussions on the art of putting because it eliminated two important variables. Now, golfers could concentrate all their attention on assessing the effect of wind, slope, grain, and surface conditions, which are enough complications without having to take differing sizes and weights of ball into consideration.

Down the ages, golfers had played with three other main types of ball. The art of

making balls with stitched leather covers stuffed with wool or feathers was well established in Roman times, and these featheries were the standard ammunition for the gentlemen golfers from the earliest times, as we can deduce from the records of shipments of sheepskin leather balls stuffed with cows' hair from Holland to Scotland from the year 1486 onward. Golf was also a popular pastime among the commoners in Scotland: indeed, the game was forbidden by two royal decrees during the fifteenth century because men were neglecting their archery practice in favor of the links. That would never do because they had to keep their military skills up to scratch as they were liable at any time to be drafted into a citizens' army to repulse the English invaders and other marauders. Featheries would have been prohibitively expensive for such artisan golfers, each one costing the equivalent of a week's wages, and so they played with balls turned from finely grained hardwoods such as beech, box, and elm. Only one such golf ball has survived to this day, but it can be dated with some accuracy because it was driven deep into the mud beneath a wooden pile that formed part of the foundations of a building erected on the Amsterdam waterfront in 1589. It is slightly larger than modern golf balls and weighs rather less.

A perfectly smooth sphere has hopeless aerodynamic properties, thus a golf ball without dimples never becomes airborne, dipping disconcertingly soon after the initial impetus off the clubface and going nowhere. So those wooden balls would have been pretty useless until they had become knocked about a bit, either by deliberate roughing of the surface or through the wear and tear of play. Similarly, the featherie's stitched seams broke up the surface smoothness sufficiently to give the ball its required lift, and by all accounts it was a highly effective golf ball. There are authenticated records of drives well over 300 yards with featherie balls, albeit in favorable conditions, and good players expected to drive the ball in the range of 175 to 220 yards as a matter of course.

To achieve comparable performances with wooden balls they would have to have been weighted. In both cases, because only surface irregularities made the balls effective, they must have been unsuitable for precise putting. Holing out, we may surmise, was in the early days of the game a hit-and-miss business indeed.

Golf underwent a major revolution in 1848 with the introduction of the gutta percha ball, the guttie. Gutta percha is a natural substance, the sap of a tree that can be tapped in the same manner as rubber. On exposure to the air gutta percha becomes as hard as fireclay, but it becomes malleable again when placed in boiling water. After a few false starts while the pioneers learned by trial and error that a smooth surface produces dismal results, the guttie proved to be a winner. It was cheap, easily produced in quantity in iron molds, and, if it became chipped or broken in play, the pieces could be recycled by boiling them up and remolding them. As the ballmakers evolved more sophisticated surface patterns, the guttie took on consistent aerodynamic qualities, enabling golfers such as Allan Robertson and Young Tom Morris to employ spin to control the flight of their shots. In addition, the guttie retained its symmetry, so the hit-and-hope business of putting could finally begin its metamorphosis into the art form we know today.

The first specialist putter was Willie Park, Jr., who won the British Open Championships of 1887 and 1889, maintaining a proud family record established by his father and his uncle Mungo. Willie coined the phrase "The man who can putt is a match for anyone," and he also wrote the first handbook of putting. He gives a graphic account of how he acquired his touch with the putter:

When I was a boy I used to be in the habit of playing with other companions on one of the putting greens of Musselburgh links. Here we spent a large part of our spare moments putting for halfpennies. We usually played until darkness stopped us; and then, taking the key (needless to say without sanction) of my father's club-shop, we would adjourn to these premises to continue our sport on the red brick floors. The holes were made by scooping out a slight hollow in the middle of the chosen bricks, and to overcome the darkness we hit upon the idea of placing a lighted halfpenny candle as flag staff at each hole. This putting, besides being unique, was, as can be well imagined, also extremely difficult. Never in any match or practice have I had a putt which needed as much skill as those I played on that red brick floor.

Guttie balls came in a variety of sizes, weights, and surface patterns, as well as varying degrees of hardness, and one of the charms of golf during the second half of the nineteenth century was unquestionably the diversion of ballmanship. The golfer experimented to discover the size and weight that best suited him, after which came the delicate task of judging when a ball was ripe. Fresh from the mold the ball was relatively soft and had to be put away to harden, but there came a point when it reached its optimal consistency and was ready for play. So before going to the course, the golfer had to repair to his store of new golf balls and bounce them one by one on a hard floor to find the ones that had reached their peak. If a ball was too soft it felt dead on the clubface and if too hard it was as unresponsive as a stone. The ball had to be a good "stotter," as the expression had it, and a ball's behavior off the face of the putter was as important as its flight from a full drive in determining what constituted a good stotter.

The guttie was a good ball for putting, so much so that some golfers believe it was easier to putt than the modern ball, especially in holing out from that nervous range between four and six feet. Being less resilient than a rubber-core ball, it could be struck firmly on short putts and consequently held its line well. But that virtue

For the want of a nail...

Half a roll away from glory. By this margin Ed Sneed failed on the final green to win the 1979 Masters.

could not long prevail against the manifold advantages of the Haskell ball, which came along at the turn of the century.

Coburn Haskell, of Cleveland, Ohio, deserves the unstinted gratitude of every golfer for his invention of a method of winding elastic thread under tension around a solid core, thus giving the world the rubber golf ball. Others had tried to incorporate rubber in gutta percha balls, producing a breed of generally unsatisfactory balls called putties. But the Haskell swept all opposition aside, in the wake of a sneaky trick pulled at the British Open Championship of 1902.

The first Haskells were just coming into Britain at that time and were being loudly castigated by the traditionalists who had been brought up on the trusty guttie. At the Royal Liverpool club before the 1902 championship the Scot Sandy Herd, a well-known and authoritative figure in golf, tried a Haskell and roundly condemned the newcomer as being altogether too lively off the clubface for accurate golf. That settled the issue for any waverers; if Sandy Herd said the new ball was hopeless, then that was that. Everyone played guttie balls—except for Sandy Herd. He used his one precious Haskell. A contemporary account tells that by the end of the championship, the windings of Herd's ball were trailing behind it like the tail feathers of a rooster. But the canny Scot won the championship, and the Haskell ball was launched as the most significant development in golf since the invention of the guttie.

In contrast to the history of the golf ball, the story of the putter is tranquil. The first putters were slightly scaled-down versions of the other clubs, with banana-shaped wooden heads weighted with lead. Such clubs are still being made and used to this day by craftsmen who employ the traditional tools and techniques to shape the heads and fit ram's-horn inserts with square pegs driven into round holes, surely the origin of the common expression for someone who is out of his element. The iron-headed putting cleek then became popular for use with the gut-

tie ball, and they too survive, except that nowadays we call them blade putters. The modern putter may be a marvel of balance and precision engineering, the ultimate expression of scientific research and high technology, but truth to tell it is not much different from the putters forged by cleekmakers in St. Andrews, Musselburgh, and Leith well over a hundred years ago.

If putters have changed little in form down the centuries, it is not for lack of human ingenuity. Probably no other area of golf has been subjected to more attention by inventors and researchers, a high proportion of whom have almost surely been clinically certifiable if judged by the weird and wonderful contraptions they have submitted to the governing bodies for approval: putters with wheels, putters with complex arrangements of prisms and mirrors to act like gun-sights, putters with spring-loaded striking surfaces, putters with plumb bobs, one-handed putters no more than a foot long, putters with shafts coiled like writhing snakes. The United States Golf Association and the Royal and Ancient have cupboards bulging with these expressions of forlorn hopes for a magic wand. Alas, one of the oldest truths in the game cannot be denied: the fault—or the magic—lies not in the club but in the golfer who is wielding it.

The era of giving personal names to individual clubs has long passed, more's the pity, but a few putters have become part of golf's heritage. Willie Park, Jr.'s, putter, "Old Pawky," with which he justly claimed to be the match for anyone, now has a place of honor in the Woking Golf Club, a few miles south of London. Even more famous is "Calamity Jane," another blade putter and a vital contributor to the Grand Slam of Bobby Jones. Calamity Jane now rests in a glass display case at the Augusta National Golf Club, home of the Masters Tournament, which Jones founded.

For many years golfers swore by the aphorism that driving is an art, approach play a science, and putting an inspiration. The man who laid that notion dead was a somewhat unlikely hero, Walter J. Travis, an American of Australian birth who did not take up golf until the age of thirty-five. He was a slight, round-shouldered man with a somewhat dour mien and a grouchy disposition. What he had in his favor, and in superabdundance, were application, dedication, and an acutely analytical mind. The idea of putting as an exercise in inspiration was totally foreign to his beliefs. Walter Travis made a deep study of the mechanics of putting and from his researches developed a distinctive technique that was devastatingly effective. After winning the U. S. Amateur Championship three times, he set out to become the first foreign player to win the British Amateur, at Sandwich in 1904, when he was aged forty-three. The trip started badly. Travis had allowed himself plenty of time to practice before the championship, but day by day his game deteriorated. Worst of all, his putting completely deserted him. To make matters worse, he was met with hostility by the championship officials, who refused him permission to change the thoroughly unsatisfactory caddie who had been allotted to him, and the galleries responded to his aloof personality with their own frigidity.

On the eve of the championship, thinking he had nothing to lose and in the sure knowledge that he could not use his own putter, Travis borrowed a friend's. It was a center-shafted mallet type, known as a Schenectady putter, and in Travis's hands it became truly a magic wand. He went through the preliminary rounds like an avenging angel, and in a dour final against the big-hitting Ted Blackwell he putted his way to victory. It was not a popular win, being greeted in silence at the moment of triumph and a short while afterward by the banning of center-shafted putters in Royal and Ancient competitions. This move was widely and properly seen as an example of sour grapes on the part of the R and A and as a stuffy reproof to Travis for seeking an unfair advantage with his newfangled club. That ungracious act was not remedied for half a century, when the ban was finally re-

pealed. Nevertheless, it was a remarkable victory for a man who had been playing golf for only eight years and most of all a personal triumph of the human spirit over adversity. This was a performance as significant to the game of golf as Roger Bannister's four-minute mile was to athletics. Travis shattered a great many preconceptions about putting and gave to golf the psychological release that enabled others to pursue unprecedented standards that would eventually turn this seemingly simple exercise into an art form.

The concept of the putting green as a sacrosanct area of prepared turf, to be used exclusively for putting, grew with increasing force during those years of progressively moving the teeing area farther and farther from the hole. All this happened during the period when individual clubs made their own rules, but the Society of St. Andrews Golfers was made up of the great innovators and acknowledged arbiters of the game long before they accepted the responsibility for the official regulation of golf.

It was St. Andrews that toughened the challenge of its course by incorporating four of its twenty-two holes into two, thus establishing the convention of eighteen holes as the norm for a golf course. The club used two holes on its huge double greens, and the appointment of Old Tom Morris as its first greenkeeper and professional meant that those greens were kept in prime condition. Thus when the other clubs petitioned St. Andrews, by now the Royal and Ancient Golf Club, to take over as the governing body of golf, and the club formally defined separate greens and teeing areas, it was simply making its own established practices the rules for all clubs.

These changes opened the way for advances in course design. In the earliest times, golfers played wherever the fancy took them, learning through experience which routes made for the best sport and thereby which holes to formalize. The emergence of the greenkeeper-professional provided a source of expert advice and experience, and as new clubs came into being they commissioned this new breed of professional golfer to visit the site and lay out the course. Such work initially consisted simply of establishing the route, the pro walking over the land and fitting the holes into its natural features and setting markers where the greens were to be established. There was seldom any question of altering the topography in any way, and construction was limited to the removal of shrubbery to form the "fairgreen" (fairway) and to rudimentary preparation of the greens.

The growing popularity of the game meant that golf had to move to inland sites that bore little relationship to the traditional linksland. Then the designers had to work with woodland, clay, and loam instead of sand-based soils, and these fresh challenges stimulated the growth of the specialist course designer. Thus was created the profession of golf course architect, a man who needed much more than golfing expertise to perform his task. Above all, he had to have vision to see the golfing potential of his site, then skill and resources to alter the landscape, a considerable undertaking with only horsepower and rudimentary implements at his disposal. The best of this new breed of architect produced courses recognized as masterpieces to this day, and, although mechanical equipment has vastly increased the scope for earth-moving and landscaping, architectural principles have not greatly changed. The one significant advance is that today's architects devote much more attention to the strategic and cosmetic planning of their courses, but essentially they work according to principles established by those early pioneers.

The first of those new inland courses may not have been created in Britain at all, but in Charleston, South Carolina, in 1786. There is natural linksland in the area, but early Charleston golfers chose to play over a city park, Harleston's Green, which has long since given way to urban development. Not only that first golf club but golf itself then disappeared from American soil,

not to be reintroduced until a hundred years later. This time, however, the golf virus developed into a raging epidemic. The first designers were immigrants from Scotland, and they were quickly superseded by native-born designers, who were largely instrumental in establishing the principles of the new profession.

What are these principles? Most architects, and most golfers for that matter, would go along with the thirteen articles enunciated by Alistair Mackenzie, the Scottish doctor who forsook medicine to become a golf club secretary and then gave up golf administration for his true avocation of designing courses. Just three of his courses, Augusta National, Cypress Point, and Royal Melbourne, are sufficient to establish his credentials. He decreed:

1. The ideal course should be arranged in two loops where possible.
2. There should be at least four one-shot holes, two or three drive-and-pitch holes, and a large proportion of good two-shot holes.
3. There should be little walking between greens and tees.
4. Greens and fairways should be sufficiently undulating, but there should be no hill climbing.
5. Every hole should have a different character.
6. There should be a minimum of blindness for the approach shots.
7. The course should have beautiful surroundings. All artificial features should be so natural in apearance that a stranger is unable to distinguish them from nature itself.
8. There should be a sufficient number of heroic carries from the tee, but the course should be so arranged that an alternative route is always open to the weaker player.
9. There should be an infinite variety of strokes required to play the various holes.
10. There should be a complete absence of the annoyance caused by the necessity to search for lost balls.

Is it a bird? Is it a plane?

The art of putter levitation and a mystified Lanny Wadkins.

SWEARING
by Lord Balfour
Prime Minister of Great Britain

Expletives more or less vigorous directed against himself, the ball, the club, the wind, the bunker, and the game are the most usual safety valve for the fury of the disappointed golfer. But bad language is fortunately much gone out of use; and in any case, the resources of profanity are not inexhaustible. Deeds, not words, are required in extreme cases to meet the exigencies of the situation; and, as justice, prudence, and politeness all conspire to shield his opponent from physical violence, it is on the clubs that under these circumstances vengeance most commonly descends. Most players content themselves with simply breaking the offending weapon against the ground.

But some persons there are whose thirst for revenge cannot be satisfied by any such rapid or simple process. I have been told of one gentleman who threw the offending club on the ground, and then with his niblick proceeded to punish it with

Creeping up from behind on an unsuspecting Hale Irwin.

Vertical take-off from the human launching pad of Juli Inkster.

Is it a guided missile?

piecemeal destruction, breaking its shaft into small pieces very much as criminals used to be broken on the wheel. Even this procedure seemed inadequate to one infuriated golfer of whom I have heard. A shaft, be it broken into ever so many fragments, can be replaced and the implement be as good as new. Nothing less than destroying both head and shaft can insure its final disappearance from the world of Golf. The club must not merely be broken, but must be destroyed, and from its hated remnants no new race must be permitted to arise for the torment and discomfiture of succeeding generations of golfers. This perfect consummation can, it is said, be attained by holding the club upright, the head resting on the ground, then placing one foot upon it and kicking it with the other, just at the point where the head and shaft are bound together. By this simple expedient (which I respectfully commend to the attention of all short-tempered golfers) a "root-and-branch" policy may be effectually carried out by destroying at one stroke both the essential parts of the club. It is better to smash your clubs than to lose your temper.

A. J. Balfour.

The one that nearly got away—from Joanne Carner.

Moment of blast-off for Graham Marsh's feckless club.

The putter's revenge, in hot pursuit of Tommy Horton.

11. The course should be so interesting that even the plus-handicap man is constantly stimulated to improve his game in attempting shots he has been hitherto unable to play.

12. The course should be so arranged that the high-handicap player enjoys his round.

13. The course should be equally good during winter and summer. The texture of the greens and fairways should be perfect, and the approaches should have the same consistency as the greens.

Most of these points are concerned with the course as a whole, and it might be thought, therefore, that they have no place in a book devoted to putting. Consequently, this is as good a place as any to introduce an instructional element, for the lesson to be imparted is so vital—and so fundamental—that until it is thoroughly assimilated all the rest is irrelevant.

The golfer is constantly being programmed to believe that putting is something apart from golf. The language of golf—"a game within a game," "drive for show, putt for dough"—suggests that putting is an activity divorced from the rest of golf. The rules, with their definition of the putting green and their special regulations for play on the green, reinforce this impression. Even our implements imply a clear distinction, with the putter the odd man out among matching woods and irons.

Historically, the great players have been among the worst offenders in separating the game into two entities, golf and putting. Most of them have fiercely resented the slightest criticism of their abilities as strikers but willingly—almost avidly at times—confessed themselves to be downright incompetent putters. For instance, if they drive badly they go to the driving range to cure the problem, but if they putt badly they are as likely to go to the pro shop to buy a new putter. No one has ever satisfactorily explained this Jekyll-and-Hyde phenomenon among golfers, although the resentment of criticism is easily understood

when you consider that the tournament professional survives by confidence and so must never allow thoughts of his own fallibility to penetrate his consciousness, from whatever source.

And that, of course, is the reason for what outsiders often think is boorish criticism by great players of golf courses, or golf course conditions, after a bad round. To excuse a bad score, the player blames the fairways and the greens and the bunker sand and the spectators and the weather and even—in the case of P. G. Wodehouse's famous character—"the uproar of the butterflies in the adjoining meadow." In short, he has to find some external reason for failure because the alternative—that his golf might have been at fault—is intolerable.

Such negative thoughts can be destructive and thus, if allowed to fester in the golfer's mind, can eventually ruin his career; he has to believe in his prowess because that faith in himself in his greatest asset. If such self-delusion is necessary, why does it not extend to include putting? Here we run into difficulties because we are seeking rational reasons for irrationality. Among the world's finest golfers there have probably been no more than a dozen who were prepared to claim: "I am an excellent putter." One possible explanation for this reticence lies in the murky depths of the psyche among the lumber of superstitions and phobias most of us accumulate. Not entirely without justification, putting is associated with luck, and it may be that golfers dare not entertain notions of being good putters lest they tempt the fates. A more prosaic explanation, of course, is that a good proportion of golfers are indifferent putters and thus feel they would be placing too great a strain on their powers of self-deception to pretend otherwise. The point is that one way or another, a wedge has been driven into the game, separating the striking from the putting, and it is important that this wedge be removed. To play our best, we must see golf as an entity, with any one shot no more and no less important than any of the others. We must erase the concept of putting as a different game that must be played at the end of every hole, after the *real* business has been completed.

The game of golf should not be seen in sequential terms: first the driver, then the iron, then the horrible business of holing out. Such an attitude leads to golf by automatic pilot, devoid of the essential element of approaching each hole as an intellectual challenge. What the golfer must always remember is that the object of the game is *to get the ball into the hole in the fewest number of strokes,* an idea so basic and obvious that many golfers overlook it. Their approach is to look at the distance marker on the tee—say 390 yards, par 4—and automatically respond with the calculation: drive and seven-iron. But if the initial inquiry as the golfer steps onto the tee is to ask himself what is the most sensible way to get the ball into the hole in the fewest number of strokes, then a vast array of possibilities present themselves for consideration. And that consideration will naturally start with the position of the flagstick on the green, its proximity to bunkers or other hazards, the best line of approach, and the shot calculated to get the ball closest to the flag. Now, working backward from that objective, the routine drive and seven-iron may well seem ridiculous. The strategy for getting down in the fewest number of strokes, as opposed to blindly following convention, might well suggest a four-iron short of the pond, followed by a five-iron across the water to the invitingly tilted green. Thus, properly evaluated, putting becomes an intrinsic element in every shot, influencing the choice of both tee shot and approach shot.

Putting is omnipresent. It is not a formality at the end of the hole but a vital strand running throughout the play of the course. For instance, you might think that the condition of the tees could not possibly affect the putting, but it can, and does. Every part of golf is closely interrelated, and that is one reason why putting statistics are a form of madness. All statistics are a form of madness—or at least of mendacity according to Mark Twain—but in the case of putting, they are dangerous madness because they perpetuate the fallacy that putting is a game apart. Counting how many putts you take is exactly the same as recording the number of times you hit your six-iron, and you would get some very strange looks if you started doing that. So, the first task is to assimilate the putt into the family of golf, affording it equal status to all the other shots, believing in it with the same faith that we afford to the mighty drive and the trusty iron. Once a golfer has welcomed his putter in out of the cold, he is well on the way to exorcising his fears of the black art.

Confidence is the key to golf at all levels; everyone knows that. The golfer who believes in his own abilities will always beat an opponent who is assailed by self-doubt. It is one thing to identify the secret of golf, however, and quite another to acquire that precious confidence. In this respect, the game may have lost a valuable asset in the name of progress. In the last century clubs were hand-built by craftsmen who checked their work at every stage by hefting the club in their experienced hands. If the balance seemed a little off, they would shave a fraction from the head, or rub down the shaft, until the club felt right, with the balance and flex of the shaft adjusted to perfection. Of course, no two clubs were the same, and the golfer might waggle dozens of clubs—hundreds even, in the case of meticulous professionals—before finding a mashie that was exactly "right." The same process had to be followed in acquiring a driver, a spoon, a cleek, a mid-iron, a mashie-niblick, a niblick, and a putter. And because the hickory shaft was susceptible to breakage, all serious golfers had to furnish themselves with spares. So with both balls and clubs the golfer was obliged to invest considerable time and care in the selection of his equipment, and this created a very close bond between the player and his implements.

It was common, as we have seen, for golfers to give pet names to their clubs. In this age of scientific golf it may seem excessively fanciful for a golfer to call his pitching wedge "Faith," as in the case of a well-known amateur player, on the grounds that faith can move mountains. But we can well understand how that player felt a rapport with that niblick, and how his confidence must have been brimming as he told his caddie: "This looks like a job for Faith."

The golfer of today could never achieve such a relationship with a mass-produced set of matching clubs, all stamped with impersonal numbers. Tournament professionals are almost invariably under contract to play a particular brand of clubs, which makes it very difficult to build a bond of affection for, say, the six-iron. Woods, wedges, and putters are often excluded from such contracts, which gives some scope to make romantic attachments, although few pros these days have such close relationships with their clubs as the South African champion Bobby Locke, probably the finest putter of the modern era. Locke's putter was almost a part of himself, to the point that he would never leave it in his golf bag overnight. That trusty blade went back to the hotel with Locke and spent the night in the safety of his bedroom. That club was as precious to him as a Stradivarius to a virtuoso violinist, and there is not the slightest doubt that a large part of his success on the greens was due to his love for that putter. That inanimate combination of wood and metal give him confidence because of his affection for it; he knew he could put his trust in it.

With or without statistics, we can see that putting standards have risen in recent years. The commonly expressed belief that golfers are getting better every year may be a valuable propaganda exercise for promoting tournaments, but the validity of such claims is doubtful. There is no objective evidence to support such statements, and in subjective terms it seems absurd to assert that modern golfers strike the ball better than Bobby Jones, Ben Hogan, and Byron Nelson. But scores are coming down fractionally, and there is no doubt that better putting performances are responsible for this improvement. Partly, these improved scores are attributable to an increasingly enlightened attitude to putting following the example of Walter Travis and his like. But mostly it is because of advances in greenkeeping techniques and much better quality control of golf balls.

The preparation of greens is a subject that would take a book to explore, and we will go into it in some depth later. The improvement in ball manufacture was stimulated by the velocity and distance restrictions imposed by the governing bodies. Previously, the main impetus in golf ball research had been devoted to the quest for ever greater distance in response to the most powerful factor of golf psychology, the urge to open the shoulders and fire the ball mighty distances. Once a limitation was imposed on distance, however, the ballmakers turned their attention to the vital but less glamorous areas of consistency, durability, and appearance.

During the era of the distance wars it was astonishing how high a proportion of golf balls were misshapen or off-balance. The New Zealander Bob Charles, the best left-handed player in modern international golf, was, in his prime, also the finest putter. He saw the long game as no more than a preliminary exercise, a method of getting the ball onto the green as economically as possible in preparation for real golf, the specialized game and the very heart of the competition: putting. His whole approach to golf was therefore concentrated on putting, and he went to extreme lengths to furnish himself with golf balls suitable for putting. He tested every ball individually and counted himself fortunate if he found two balls in a box of twelve that were fit for his purpose. Faulty balls were rejected for two main reasons: either for being out of balance or for not being perfectly spherical.

A simple ring test is sufficient to test a ball for shape. A ball should just brush the metal when passed through a ball ring. You then rotate the ball through ninety degrees and repeat the experiment. If this time the ball sticks in the ring, or drops through without touching the sides, it is out of shape. If the distortion is fractional, a matter of a mere coat of paint, the effect on the roll of the ball will not be significant. A ball that is out of balance, however, is a much more serious proposition.

Rolling a ball on a perfectly flat surface, such as a pool table, making sure to rotate it through different axes, is the easiest way to observe the eccentric roll that reveals that it is out of balance. A more scientific method is to prepare a solution whose specific gravity is almost the same as that of the ball, allowing the ball to float with just a small area, about the size of a fingernail, above the surface. Once the ball has settled down and is perfectly stationary, put a mark in the center of the exposed area. Then give the ball a spin and allow it to settle again. If it comes to rest with that mark above the surface again, you may be sure that the ball has a bias that will pull the putt off a true line. Putting is difficult enough without the ball having its own built-in sense of misdirection.

Rogue golf balls may be the exception rather than the norm these days, but standards of quality control vary from maker to maker, and the serious golfer is advised to experiment with different brands and give his loyalty to the ball that has the highest pass rate in the symmetry and balance tests. The mind reels at the thought of the thousands of golfers who must have been driven to distraction and frenzied experimentation with different putting styles during a round when the real culprit was a ball whose core was off center.

It may seem excessively persnickity to test every golf ball before you play it, and even the suggestion of preliminary trials of different brands could appear to be taking the game altogether too seriously. But the justification for such a policy is that it removes one area of doubt from the mind of the golfer, freeing him to concentrate on the business at hand. In other words, it is just one more aid to confidence. The Englishman Arthur Lees, a Ryder Cup veteran and longtime professional at Sunningdale, once narrowly missed a twenty-five-footer and commanded: "Caddie, throw that ball back to me." Lees inspected the errant missile with a scowl of disdain and commented: "I knew the bugger wasn't round," and threw it into the bushes. That's confidence.

The word "par" has a precise mathematical meaning in golf, and so it has come to be used universally as the standard against which performance is measured. It is not entirely suitable for this purpose because it is demonstrably absurd to call a man the leader when he is on the seventeenth hole and his nearest rival in relation to par is playing the second. The most you can say is that he is the leader among the group playing the seventeenth, although we all go along with the illogical system. Of course, this does not really matter because everyone understands full well that the term "leader" in a golf tournament is a necessarily imprecise title and divorced from its usual meaning in the context of, say, a four-hundred-meter running race. Par is a far more dangerous word when we program it into our calculations as the target score for an individual hole, and as such it is best excluded from the golfer's mind.

Take the case of a long hole at about the limit for a par-four being played into a strong headwind. Regardless of the figures on the card, that hole is now a three-shotter, so it is foolish to castigate yourself for dropping a stroke to par when you mark down a five and still more dangerous if that experience prompts the urgent thought that you must quickly regain the lost stroke. The same applies in reverse, with a short par-five and a following gale: the golfer must resist any feelings of self-congratulation when he makes a four. Ela-

Purgatory...

Conductor on the podium,
Gary Player with gallery control finger

Altogether ... NOW!
Let the hosannahs ring forth across the course.

Ben Crenshaw. The Stroke ...

Pause for outside assistance—

and now the celebration.

and Paradise

God is a Mexican, as Lee Trevino is fond
of observing.

With visor lowered at half mast,
Philip Parkin grieves.

Back in the old routine, buck and wing
by Sandra Palmer.

Jack Nicklaus. When you miss a few the
successes are so sweet.

tion and despair are equally treacherous allies to the golfer. And the worst place of all for the par mentality is on the green.

According to the laws of the Medes and Persians (neither of whom could play a lick, but that's incidental), on a par-72 golf course the regulation performance is 36 shots from tee to green and 36 putts. From this it might be thought that 36 putts is a pretty satisfactory standard. After all, that is what the book says. The truth, however, is that any tournament professional who regularly takes 36 putts a round is destined for a career selling hot dogs.

A striking example of the importance of ignoring par was demonstrated by Gary Koch in the Doral Open of 1983. He had 171 shots from tee to green, which is 27 over par and not terribly impressive. But, he had only 100 putts, or 44 under par for strokes on the green, and he won by 5 shots with an aggregate of 17 under par. That shows the irrelevance of where you hit your shots; all that matters is the total at the end of the day. If Koch had allowed himself to become depressed by the realization that he was dropping seven shots a round with his long game, he surely could never have marched on to a famous victory.

The tyranny of par is particularly virulent on the greens. The golfer does not have a ration of two putts per green, and that injunction applies as equally to the thirty-handicapper as it does to the professional. The handicap player should regard his allocation of strokes purely as an allowance for the long game. There are many good reasons why golfers need handicap strokes for the long game if they are to compete on level terms with the hotshots, but on the greens all men are equal. There is no reason whatsoever why the worst striker in the world should not compete at putting on even terms with the mightiest champions. That four-and-one-quarter-inch hole is the great leveler before which all men are equal. You may think that to be an exaggeration, a gross overstatement of the case, because, after all, professionals are able to spend many hours every day hon-

ing their technique so they must have a huge advantage. Well, listen to one of the greatest putters of the modern era, Bob Charles, on that subject: "Method or technique is less than 5 percent of putting." So dismiss par from your thinking and reprogram your calculations to a more positive formula: the correct number of putts that should be taken by a good putter is ONE PER GREEN. What a much better-balanced game of golf it would be if we could all get within shouting distance of that standard.

In an average round of seventy-two a professional might use his putter for thirty-two strokes, his driver for twelve, and spread another twenty-eight strokes among his other twelve clubs. A number of conclusions can be drawn from those figures: that putting offers far and away the most fruitful area for a golfer of any standard to improve his game; that golf is a lopsided game; and, perhaps, that the emphasis on putting is becoming too marked for the good of golf.

Twenty years ago on the PGA Tour there were fifteen to twenty potential winners in every tournament. Of course, that is not to say there were no surprise winners; there were, as there will always be because of the natural law which proclaims that every dog will have his day. But generally speaking, the first prizes were claimed by a small elite of regular winners. On other professional circuits around the world, such as they were, the lists of probable winners were even smaller. Today, the game has progressed to the point that there might be fifty potential winners in the field for a U.S. tour event, which is not to say necessarily that golf standards are rising. Nobody today is scoring the way Byron Nelson did in his prime, striking the ball with the accuracy of Ben Hogan, or mastering every facet of golf in the manner of Bobby Jones. But the standard is undeniably very high, and there are many, many more players at that standard. The result is that dozens of players are hitting about the same number of shots from tee to green, and that inevitably means that golf tournaments are said to be becoming, in effect, putting competitions. Is that what golf should be? As we have seen earlier, it most certainly is not what golf *used* to be. Of course, the specialist putter must enjoy the advantage of his skill. There can be no question of that. The question at issue is whether the virtuoso iron player is being properly rewarded for his special skills in the modern game.

Consider the example of two golfers, Striker and Putter, who have both hit fine drives down the fairway. Striker now holds up a fine two-iron against the crosswind and pitches his ball twenty feet from the flag. Putter flails away with his three-wood, and the ball finishes fifteen yards wide of the green. With the modern broad-soled wedge it is little more than a formality for Putter to pitch up a few feet from the flagstick and hole out for a four. Striker's approach shot has certainly given him a better chance to make three, but even so it is not a very good chance. In fact, thanks to research by the United States Golf Association in the U.S. Open of the putting probabilities by champion golfers, we can quantify Striker's chances. From that range, he will succeed only once in seven attempts. Is that just reward for his superior approach play? Such experiences provide little encouragement for golfers to work on their strokemaking.

The question is not raised in an attempt to promote a golfing revolution, with armies of enraged fanatics storming Golf House and demanding holes the size of buckets. But it is a subject worthy of serious debate—not to mention a stimulus to working on the putting stroke.

The statistical research mentioned above provides an interesting insight into the level of putting performance of the leading professionals. Jack Reddy, USGA scoring analyst, calculated that the winner of the U.S. Open Championship must roll a 75-foot putt within 4 1/2 feet of the hole and that this rate of accuracy must improve in proportion as the approach putts become

shorter. From 40 feet his putt will finish within 2.4 feet of the hole, and from 30 feet within 1.8 feet. That represents an impressive standard of approach putting. But when it comes to holing out, the champion proves that he is all too mortal. His gimme length is 2 1/2 feet; he holes everything from that range. But he has a success rate of only 50 percent from 7 feet, and by the time he gets back to 20 feet, as we have seen, he needs two putts six times out of seven attempts.

These figures represent averages, of course, and Reddy points out that the champion will have at least one hot round when his putting figures are well below the norm. The best recorded putting performance on the PGA Tour was 18 by Sam Trahan, at Whitemarsh Valley Country Club, in the last round of the Philadelphia Golf Classic of 1979. The following year George Archer clipped five strokes off the four-round record when he needed only 94 putts in the Sea Pines Heritage Classic at Harbour Town Golf Links—and still did not win the tournament. And, of course, such freakishly low putting rounds are mostly the result of wayward approach play, requiring the golfer to be chipping and pitching close to the flag from off the green. For example, if Archer had hit every green in regulation that week he would have had a total of 238, instead of his actual aggregate of 284. Likewise, Trahan would have scored 54!

One of the reasons why putting generates such spirited debates about its excessive importance, or otherwise, with the battle lines drawn between those who are not very good at it and those with a gift, is probably because of what appears to be the inherent injustice of the art. A tap-in of half an inch counts the same as a drive of 280 yards, perhaps skillfully held up against a stiff crosswind, and even though both count as one stroke, it is patently absurd to equate the two in terms of accomplishment. Therein, however, lies both the challenge and the charm of putting, because it is entirely reasonable in terms of skill to equate the *previous* putt with a full drive. Perhaps it was a twenty-footer across subtly opposed slopes, with that same stiff crosswind complicated by a suspicion of grain. The player who reads that putt correctly and then executes a stroke to deliver the ball securely into the hole is due every bit as much reward as the golfer who splits the fairway from the tee. And that is why the half-inch tap-in must count as one stroke: because it is the distinction that measures the gulf between genius and the merely competent.

Never was such genius more graphically rewarded than in the 1961 PGA Championship at Olympia Fields in Chicago, when Jerry Barber was four strokes behind Don January with three holes to play. On the sixteenth green Barber holed a curling twenty-footer for a birdie. On the seventeenth he holed from forty feet for another birdie. At the last hole Barber pulled his approach shot, and, although the ball found the left side of the green, it was sixty feet from the hole. Down went the putt, and the two players were tied, with Barber winning the next day's playoff. Nobody, not even January, could argue that Barber was anything but a worthy winner, thanks to his exceptional putting.

Putting was also the decisive factor in another PGA championship, in 1932, when the championship was contested at match-play. Al Watrous was nine up with thirteen holes to play when he conceded a six-foot putt to Bobby Cruikshank for a half. With such a comfortable lead, Watrous had every right to feel magnanimous. Cruikshank, however, holed a twenty-footer for a winning birdie at the seventh and also took the eighth and ninth, where Watrous three-putted. Cruikshank's putting then became inspired, including a seventy-five-footer at the fifteenth and another monster on the home green that squared the match. They halved the first three extra holes and then, at the fourth, or the fortieth hole in the match, the tide that had been running so strongly in Cruikshank's favor seemed to turn. The hole was a short par-three, and Cruikshank overshot the green, finishing on a bank. Watrous's tee shot stopped two feet from the cup. Cruikshank putted down short from the bank, missed with his next putt, and then holed out with his fourth stroke. Watrous slid his downhill two-footer past the hole about a foot, and then, with his mind still half wondering whether Cruikshank would concede the tiddler, he left it short of the hole. So that was a half and Cruikshank won the match—and one of the most implausible victories in the history of championship golf—at the fifth extra hole.

There are morals aplenty in those two extraordinary incidents, and they will be examined in detail as together we saunter down the fairway and onto the green of the game within a game, putting.

WHERE SOFT THE FOOTSTEPS FALL

Make up your mind what you are going
to do, then go ahead and do it.
                                    —Bobby Locke

Serious golfers well understand how important it is for them to know all about grass. After all, grass is the medium of their craft, and so a comprehensive knowledge of grass is as vital to them as it was for the old masters to have a thorough understanding of paints and pigments. By the time Jack Nicklaus starts a championship, he has identified every variety of grass to be found on the golf course and, given the slightest encouragement, he will recite their botanical names in passable Latin and deliver a dissertation on the properties of each species. Most other great players also lapse into horticulture from time to time, if only to the point of explaining their lack of success with a thirty-foot putt by saying that they were unsure how the ball might roll because of a small patch of *poa annua* intervening on the line to the hole.

Tournament golfers who have become course designers are justified in their preoccupation with agronomy, but for the most part the golfer who aspires to learn all about grass is wasting his time. The greatest botanist on earth does not know all about grass, nor even a fraction of all there is to be known. The reason is that there are more than five thousand varieties of grass, and new ones are being developed all the time, and that is only the start of it. Take just one of those five thousand varieties and think of it as a tribe, like, for example, the Kikuyu, which conveniently happens to be an East African tribe as well as a variety of grass. Within that tribe there are innumerable families, each with its own idiosyncracies. So, if you sow a sward of Kikuyu grass, you may well come across patches that differ markedly from the norm, just as families within the Kikuyu tribe have different characteristics.

That is just one of the complications of grassmanship. Another is that the land on which you plant the sward of Kikuyu will have variations in its organic composition—a slight deficiency of manganese here, a change of acidity there—and these will again markedly affect the grass. Thus it is absolutely hopeless for the golfer to embark on a study of grass in the academic sense, which is not to say that he should ignore the subject entirely. The single most important thing is for clubs *to ensure that their practice greens are the same as the greens on the course, with the same varieties of grass and maintained to the same standard.* Half a dozen chip shots on the fringe and a similar number of practice putts will then give the golfer all the knowledge he needs about grass for the coming round.

What a relief! We are exonerated from any duty to learn about grass. The technicalities may safely be left to the agronomists and the greenkeepers and to the herbivores who have to eat it. And when the club's grass bore—and every club has one—approaches with his catalog of complaints about hitting fliers from the fescue alongside the fifteenth fairway, we need no longer try to disguise our ignorance of what on earth he is talking about. There is neither disgrace nor handicap in not knowing about grass, and we are free to exercise our inalienable right to stifle a yawn and move along to the other end of the bar.

It is, of course, a fundamental truism of golf that if there are 50 million golfers on earth, there are 50 million golf course architects. Once again, it must be stressed that it is by no means obligatory for golfers to study architecture or to feign knowledge of that vast subject in order to play the game decently. The challenge to the golfer is not to create or improve holes but to concentrate on mastering the results of other people's labors. A healthy attitude to such technicalities was demonstrated by a member of the Royal St. George's Golf Club, who wrote in the suggestion book: "Suggest that the water on the fourteenth green be changed." That pithy comment was much more effective than any pseudo-expert dissertation on how the committee should put in a French drain.

There is a serious golfing purpose in these strictures about avoiding pretensions to technical expertise. The golfer who accepts the golf course the way he finds it is a much more effective competitor than the player who is constantly telling himself that this bunker is badly positioned, or that it is impossible to putt on greens which the idiots on the greens committee have failed to hollow-tine, or mulch, or verticut, or topdress, or roll, or double-cut. Inwardly railing against the lack of growth on the green is a sure guarantee of missing the putt. The correct approach is to observe the conditions and to allow the subconscious to compute that, since the line of the putt consists more of sand than grass, the ball must be struck more firmly than usual. It is for this reason that, although good putters naturally perform better than average putters on perfect greens, their superiority is even more marked on bad greens. The acid test of a great putter is to perform his miracles on greens that the rest of us condemn as being unplayable.

There was a time when American visitors to Britain would marvel at the velvet lawns of the country houses and the beautifully textured greens of the links golf courses. They would ask: "How do you create such superb grass?" The stock reply on such occasions was: "Oh, it's very simple. You just plant the seed and then you roll it and mow it for a hundred years." There is none of that patronizing nonsense these days when the supremacy in turf culture has passed firmly to the United States. These days, an American tournament professional will rarely encounter a truly bad green from one year's end to the next, unless he ventures abroad. Even parkland courses built on heavy clay soils boast greens that are marvels of consistency. The reasons for this are partly historical. A huge number of courses were built in America in response to the postwar boom in golf, and so the greens were created in accordance with modern specifications, with adequate drainage and irrigation and a properly balanced growing compound for the specialized varieties of golf green grasses. Another very important factor was that, though Britain has a tradition of cheap, even cheese-paring, golf, there is an even stronger tradition in the American

character of demanding the best and being prepared to pay for it.

In other areas of life it is possible to debate what may or may not constitute the "best," but in the case of golf greens, quality can be measured and defined. A good green is one on which a putt holds its true line. It is as simple as that. If a putt deviates from its true path by so much as a millimeter because of uneven growth or surface irregularities, the green is bad, period. The experience of Ken Brown is illuminating in this regard. This British Ryder Cup player had a reputation as a fine putter in Europe, and the first time he tried his luck on the American Tour he played in the Doral Open. As usual, the greens were prepared to perfection, and Brown completed his first round with only twenty-seven putts. He was bitterly disappointed with that performance, explaining that on such putting surfaces there was no reason why the ball should not go into the hole on every putt. It followed, according to his rather feverish reasoning, that he must have been at fault nine times during the round. Unfortunately, as explained later, the normal traffic of spiked golf shoes and the vagaries of the weather do introduce blemishes into the best of greens, and this is why in tournament golf the early starters on one day are sent out late for the next round.

Older American courses have been updated, in contrast again to the European experience, and it is only in recent years that there has been much of an effort to close that transatlantic gap in standards. In one respect, however, the American thrust for perfectly groomed golf courses of uniform consistency may have been counterproductive. If a player gets a perfect lie every time on a fairway of standard monoculture turf, and he faces a shot to a green of standard consistency, he is never called upon to contrive anything more ambitious in the way of shotmaking than the standard stroke of the practice range. And since there is no call to employ the skills of shaping the trajectory of his shots with hand action, he sees no need and does not work to acquire those skills. On the other hand, a golfer like Severiano Ballesteros of Spain, who served his apprenticeship on courses of wildly contrasting condition, was forced to learn ten or twenty different ways of achieving the same result, thereby becoming a more complete golfer. The balance of advantage has remained with American golfers, however, because of the superior quality of their greens. Playing on good greens all the time enables the golfer to acquire a repeating, or "grooved," stroke, a benefit denied to those who encounter greens of different consistency and quality every week. Those grooved swings and grooved putting strokes will stand up to alien conditions for a while, which explains the American domination of the British Open, but they may break down under prolonged exposure to bouncy fairways, hard greens, and blasting crosswinds. You need only to pitch to the flag once and see your ball bounce out of bounds to have your confidence eroded. Jack Nicklaus is on record as saying that if he played in Britain for six straight weeks, he fears he would lose his swing completely. No doubt the same goes for his putting stoke. Indeed, it is often the putting that goes first, and, as with a dead fish that rots from the head, so the malady spreads from the putter back through all the other clubs.

The most important factor in putting has nothing to do with the stroke; bad strokes are responsible for only a small proportion of missed putts. The root cause of the problem is misreading of the green. It is self-evident that unless the player has correctly assessed the line and speed for the putt, he will fail, no matter how smooth a stroke he makes. Similarly, indecision as to line and speed is often the main cause of infirm contact with the ball.

That some people have a natural aptitude for reading greens should not deter the less gifted. Like everything else in golf, improvement is available by sensible application and, above all, experience. Just as golf is the best exercise for golf, so putting is the best training for putting. Everyone who plays golf has experienced the strange feeling of walking onto a green, taking one glance at the ball, and knowing with absolute certainty that it is going to roll straight into the center of the hole. And it always does. The player then does not think about his grip, or his stance, or his stroke. Oblivious to such irrelevancies, he just goes up to the ball and hits it, upon which, as if running on rails, the ball dutifully clatters into the cup. It is an uncanny phenomenon, all too rare and seemingly supernatural, and the fanciful golfer can easily imagine that his hand has been guided by some external agency, and a highly benevolent one at that. The prosaic explanation is that this is one of those occasions when he has allowed his mind to work in the way it was designed to work; in other words, he has permitted his subconscious to perform naturally for once.

The purpose of this book is to restore to golfers their ability to let themselves perform as nature intended. The reason for that "supernatural" putt was that the player read the putt correctly, even without knowing he had done so, then allowed that knowledge to dictate his actions. How wonderful it would be if we could all have such putts every time. It is a tall order, but the least we can do to meet it is to eliminate some of the thoughts and actions that so completely destroy the magic of automatic response. We can, for instance, forget any ideas about reading greens through a process of mathematical calculation: "If I give the ball enough speed to die into the cup, the slope will carry it three inches to the left, and the grain will add two more inches in the same direction, and the wind will deflect it half an inch, meaning that I must borrow five and a half inches to the right of the hole." You have only to imagine a baseball player attempting such calculations as the ball hurtles toward him at a hundred miles an hour or more to realize the futility of such an exercise. The fine batter just watches the ball and lets his

brain figure out the details of speed and trajectory and then triggers his physical response in swinging the bat.

Think about the complexity of the calculations required to bring two fast-moving objects into precise contact and you get some idea of the scope of the human computer responsible for a home run. Reading a golf green is a piece of cake for such a computer, provided we can persuade ourselves to *let it get on with the job without interference.* All it needs is the full information, presented without the garnish of conscious judgments such as "How can anybody ever hole a putt on such a bad green?" or "If I blow this putt, there goes the match."

The process of programming the subconscious should be continuous and, in the case of putting, starting from the time you walk to the practice green to get the feel of the surface. You should not go out consciously to assemble "facts" from which to compile a data bank. All you have to do is *absorb* the information.

Thus you do not make a mental note to make allowances on every shot for the twenty-five-knot wind blowing from the west. Your body has millions of sensors passing this information back to headquarters, and, if you let them, they will always make the necessary allowances. Likewise, your subconscious only gets confused if you start feeding it messages about the green being bad, or the grass being too long, or there being no way to hold a shot on such a hard surface. Just be alert and get on with your putting, observing the behavior of the ball. That is all the information your subconscious needs to know.

When you start your round, and you are walking up to a green, take an impartial look at it from a distance. That general view may offer valuable information about the fall of the land. Clouds normally form in horizontal layers, and they, too, may provide helpful clues for the coming putt. The most auspicious state of mind as you walk toward the green should be one of keen anticipation of the pleasure you will experi-

ence from holing out. When you reach the green, you should continue to keep the brain in neutral. Golfers are exhorted from all sides to *concentrate.* Actually, the intensity of mental effort implied by that word is ruinous for putting. The watchword for putting is *confidence,* and a close scrutiny of every blade of grass along the line of your projected putt is a sure way of destroying confidence. The tactics should be to observe all of the elements that have a bearing on the putt in a dispassionate manner, then allow your subconscious mind to process these observations and come up with the answer in the form of a mental image of the line of the putt. Imprint that image firmly in the mind's eye, adding the refinement of the image of your ball traveling those last few inches and dropping into the hole. Once you have formulated that vision, you are as ready as you ever can be to translate it into reality.

In putting, there are four main conditions that need to be observed and fed into your mental computer. They are slope, green texture, grain, and wind, and we will go through them one by one so that you will be able to discern the significance of what you see.

The main variable is slope, and it is a matter of simple observation that the majority of golfers do not make due allowance for it. Stand by a green at any golf club on a Saturday morning and you will observe downhill putts skating well past the hole, uphill putts finishing way short of the hole, and crosshill putts in particular missing on the low side of the hole, with each roll of the ball taking it farther away from its destination. This is what the pros call missing the hole on "the amateur side," and the antidote is to allow for more break. Then if the line of aim, or borrow, is too much on the high side, the putt as it dies will at least be curling down toward the hole, leaving a shorter second putt. Missing a putt on "the professional side" is a small virtue, but there is some consolation in knowing that you erred on the correct side and thereby gave the putt a chance. There are so many

OVERLEAF
Reward for putting virtue as Ben
Crenshaw strides toward victory in the
Masters of 1984.

disappointments in golf that we must make the most of such crumbs of comfort as we can glean.

The skill of assessing the distance a putt will break on a side slope can be learned only by experience, and the most important lesson in that exercise is that a rolling ball is affected by slope in direct proportion to its speed. On a long putt across a side slope, the ball will hold its line over the first section as its sheer impetus resists the gravitational pull. But as the speed drops, the ball will become more and more affected by the slope until the last few feet of its travel, when, on a severe slope, it may well be rolling downhill at right angles to its original direction in much the same way as happens on a roulette wheel. This is why you see good golfers paying so much attention to the area close to the hole. They may look as if they had heard that someone had dropped a diamond in the grass, but actually they are trying to gather as much information as possible about the territory where the ball will be most susceptible to slope, grain, and impediment. So it is sound practice to take a good look at your line from behind the ball, then to walk forward and make another survey from about six feet short of the hole, taking care not to stand on what you suspect will be your intended line.

Side-hill putts do not travel along a regular parabola but instead trace a path more like the shape of a full drive, taking off straight from the clubface, then gradually bending in a tightening curve until they are slanting sharply downward. All this applies to putts on a uniform side slope, but as often as not, you are faced with putts that must traverse opposing slopes, first one way and then the other—the tricky double-breaker. The same principles apply. The putt will start off holding its line, uphill, downhill, and crosshill, and then as it slows, it will begin to be affected by the topography until it is fully at the mercy of the final slopes.

We learn to read greens in the same way that we learn to read books, by mastering the basic rules and then by reading and reading and reading. It is therefore foolish, as well as bad form, to bury your face in your hands, or scream at the heavens, or turn in disgust and hurl your putter into the bushes when you realize your putt is inexorably headed on the wrong line. Learn for the future by observing its progress every inch of the way. Likewise, watch the putts of your companions so that your subconscious can absorb all the relevant information and store it away for future use.

It is also a sound policy to preserve an evenhanded attitude whenever a pal sounds off with a hard-luck story: "Did you see that putt? That's downright impossible. It was right in the heart of the cup six inches from the hole!" Impossibilities do not occur in golf. The ball always behaves precisely according to the dictates of the laws of physics, thus if it took a sudden turn away from the hole, something caused it to swerve. It is no less than common courtesy to offer a "Bad luck" on such occasions, but you do not have to mean it. Look at the hole and try to discern what caused the ball's erratic behavior, and thereby become forewarned the next time you recognize the same condition.

By now, if you have played this game a while with serious intent, you will have made a conscious choice about whether you are a stroke putter, or a rap putter, or something between the two. At this point it might be well to make another important policy decision. Are you going to visualize the line to the hole and seek to direct your putt along that track? Or are you going to adhere to the school of thought which holds that all putts are straight and that the best technique is to convert your assessment of the putt into a phantom hole, or target point, and start the ball at that spot? The choice is essentially a matter of temperament and what works best for the individual. As a very broad generalization, stroke putters normally adopt the first method, while rap putters prefer to work out a target point wide of the hole and putt

straight at it. Both systems have their pluses and minuses, so it is really a question of how you "see" the putt. It is probably easier to fix the line if you have previously determined that you are going to use it like a cart path and drive your putt along it. The danger with this method is that you may be tempted to try to impart some form of swerve to the putt, by involuntarily adjusting the angle of the putter face.

Very few good putters have ever mastered the deliberate use of sidespin, although Dave Stockton, a very proficient performer on the greens, believed that he doubled the size of the hole by turning in the toe of his putter at address, or hooding the clubface as it is called, then aiming at the right edge of the hole, confident he could not miss the hole to the right. He made that style work probably more because he felt confident in it than because of any intrinsic virtue in the method. Putting to a phantom hole presents an additional complication in aiming because you have to make a secondary calculation, but, on the other hand, the actual execution of the putt is considerably easier if you have set yourself the task of hitting a dead straight putt on a flat green, albeit an imaginary one. Anyway, make your choice firmly because it will vitally affect the way you approach uphill putts. In this putt there is a distinct advantage in selecting a phantom hole directly behind the real one because you will then be emboldened to give your putt enough weight to carry it safely to its destination. If you gently dribble an uphill putt, intending the ball to topple over the front rim on its last gasp, the ball will too often wobble off course. The other advantage of a firm uphill putt—although admittedly it is a rare bonus—is that if you are on a very fast green with a severe slope, such as the eighteenth green of the Augusta National Golf Club, where the Masters is played, you could hole out with a strong putt as it horseshoes behind the hole and falls in on the return journey.

The human eye is a remarkably accurate instrument for detecting variations from the horizontal, that is, slopes on greens, *provided that* the eye can refer to a genuine horizontal such as the roof of a house or the horizon of the sea. A vertical reference, such as a pine tree, is also helpful because we are all thoroughly indoctrinated in the relationship of right angles by living in a world of rectangular buildings, doors, windows, books, newspapers, picture frames, and the like. If a picture on the wall is askew, we can detect it most easily by observing the horizontal top edge, helped by the arrangement of having two eyes set in a horizontal plane, but most of us are also pretty fair at detecting whether a vertical line is out of true if there happens to be a genuine vertical line handy as a reference. So, on seaside links—or courses that have the vertical trunks of conifer trees or buildings by the green—golfers can normally read slopes without much difficulty. But our ability to detect them is seriously impaired when we are denied true references, as in mountainous country. Then, indeed, nature sometimes conspires to confuse us. On the road to Turnberry in Scotland, there is a famous stretch where you seem to be driving steeply downhill but where, if you have been told about the phenomenon, you can stop your car and ponder the mysteries of optics as you roll smartly backward. Golf course architects of devious disposition (and which of them is not?) can build such optical illusions into their greens, but nature herself makes mischief enough to reduce our capacity to see subtle slopes. The golfer has not been born who has not at some time completely misread a putt and sent his ball rolling twenty feet past the hole because what he thought was an uphill putt proved to be a downhiller.

The plumb-bobbing system can undoubtedly be extremely useful in avoiding such embarrassments, but it must be emphasized from the start that it is not a surefire method of determining every slope in every circumstance. It performs one, and only one, function: it establishes a true vertical. If the green has just one regular slope, like the top of a tilted table, then plumb-bobbing will provide a valuable visual proof of that fact, as well as a guide as to how much the putt will break. But when the green is undulating or warped, as when you stand on a right-to-left slope with the hole cut on a left-to-right slope, the plumb-bob is likely to create more confusion than enlightenment. In any case, since the slope will always affect the putt most toward the end of its roll, when the ball is slowing down, this is the area of the green that needs to be most carefully surveyed. Thus the sensible procedure on long putts is first to stand behind your ball and make a rough judgment about the line, then pick out a spot on that line about ten feet from the hole, such as a spike mark or other blemish, then plumb-bob from that spot— again taking care not to stand on your line.

The other point to bear in mind is that plumb-bobbing will work only if your putter is suitable. A bull's-eye style of putter will hang vertically (as will some blade putters) when held lightly at the top of the grip, provided that the blade is aligned along the line of sighting. But goosenecked putters will not hang truly vertical, nor will mallet putters. So the first essential is to calibrate your putter, which is best done in the locker room. Hold the club at arm's length by the tip of the grip so that it swings freely. Close one eye and line up the shaft with a known vertical such as the edge of your locker, then rotate the putter in your fingers until the shaft is perfectly aligned with your chosen vertical. Carefully note the position of the clubhead and make sure henceforth that you hold it in this position for your plumb-bobbing.

Now for the myth of the master eye in plumb-bobbing. Someone once wrote that it was essential to employ the master eye in this exercise, and ever since all references to plumb-bobbing have stressed the vital importance of using that eye, accompa-

nied by instructions for determining which one it is. Let us lay the myth to rest once and for all. It is total balderdash. You must, it is true, use *one* eye, but which one you choose is entirely up to you. Either eye will do the job perfectly well, just as you are free to select whichever hand you prefer to hold up the putter. Some instructors advocate another unnecessary complication, namely that you must stand with your body at right angles to the ground. In other words, you have to lean one way or another according to the slope of the ground beneath your feet. You can safely forget all about that refinement, too. Just let nature take its course. After all, if you were able to detect sufficient slope for you to adopt this leaning-tower-of-Pisa stance, you would hardly need to bother with plumb-bobbing. So, just position yourself behind the mark you have selected on the green, facing the hole with your putter held at arm's length in front of you, dangling from your fingertips in perfect vertical. Using one eye, hold the club so that your mark is obscured by the lower part of the shaft. Now run your eye up the shaft, taking care not to move your head or the club. If the hole falls on the left side of the shaft, it means that the slope—and thus the break—is from right to left. It *does not* follow, however, that if the hole appears to be four inches to the left of the shaft, the putt will break into the hole if stroked four inches to the right. There are too many other factors for such precision, so what you now have is an *indication* of the direction of the slope.

In theory, an expert plumb-bobber could work his way along the line of a long putt assessing the swings and counterswings of a multiple-slope green. It would, however, be both an interminable process and a formidable task to calculate how each section of slope would affect the total roll of the ball at different speeds over a roller-coaster surface (if anyone starts such time-wasting tomfoolery in your presence the correct procedure is to make sure that he is penalized for unduly delaying play). Plumb-bobbing has its place as a guide in specific situations, but the essence of golf is human judgment, and it is to this area of reading the lie of the land, rather than to experiments as amateur surveyors, that we should devote our main attention and ultimately put our trust. Plumb-bobbing is just one aid, and a limited one, and should be used as such rather than employed indiscriminately as a way of life. As for the trend among young tournament professionals to take spirit levels with them on practice rounds so they can plot subtle slopes on the greens, they are putting their faith in false gods and, by neglecting their natural faculties, are denying themselves the chance to improve their ability to read greens by instinct. Like everything else in golf, good instruction can set you off on the right foot in reading greens, but mastery of this skill takes experience—and lots of it.

As for green texture, you should learn most of what you need to know about it during your preliminary reconnaissance on the practice green. It is a matter of common sense that wet greens are slower than the same greens when dry, thus that slopes have less effect when the turf is wet, and it follows that on sunny days the greens will become progressively faster the more they dry out. That change in pace will be tempered in some degree because the grass also grows during the day, so in practical terms the golfer has all the time he needs to adjust his weight of stroke as the round progresses without thinking about it. But there is one condition that can change character appreciably during the course of a hot day, and that is grain, or nap.

Grain is simply the way some grasses, in some conditions, tend to grow with all the blades inclined in one direction, the way the hair of a cat slopes from its head toward its tail. Golfers are frightened of grain, and in most cases it is fear of the unknown because the cause of grain is a mystery— not that this stops them from expressing firm opinions on the subject. Take a poll among the men who earn their living from golf, and you will receive a variety of authoritative replies: that grass always grows toward the rising sun, that it grows toward valleys, that it grows toward water, that it grows toward the setting sun, that it grows in the direction of the last mower to pass over it. The only common denominator in this vast mythology of grain is that all the theories are equally misleading. You can find greens, particularly in the sultry South, containing patches of grain growing toward every point of the compass.

We are not allowed to test for grain by rubbing the green surface, but it is permissible to scrape your putter lightly along the surface of the fringe that surrounds most greens. A much better way to detect the direction of the grain is simply to use your eyes. When you are looking down the grain, the surface of the green will present a distinct sheen, and when you are looking into the grain the grass will have a dull appearance. These days, improved green-keeping techniques are making great strides in the elimination of grain, but there is still plenty of it about. Indeed, in some places, such as South Africa, the grain can be potent enough to deflect a straight putt of twenty feet a good twelve inches wide of the hole. It is also common on such courses for the grain to reverse the law of gravity and for a putt to swerve uphill.

As the ball rides across the tips of the blades of grass, each individual blade contributes its nudge to throw the passing ball off course. Grain is usually far less severe in temperate climates, which is why many northern golfers ignore it altogether. But a deflection of only an inch or so can cause a putt to miss the hole, so it is always necessary to be on the lookout for grain. South Africans from Bobby Locke through Gary Player and Denis Watson have a reputation as fabulous putters, and there cannot be any doubt that their success is largely because they were brought up on grainy greens and learned early how to combat them. Moisture has a marked effect on grain. In the dewy early morning, when the grass is sappy and limber, the grain may not affect the ball too much, just as putts are deflected less by slope when

OVERLEAF
In the hush of the evening at the Oxford and
Cambridge Golfing Society's meeting at Rye.

the turf is wet. But when the sun goes to work and the grass becomes dry and bristly, grain can turn every putt into a curve ball.

It is one thing to describe the nature of grain and the horrifying way it can thwart the golfer but quite another to prescribe remedies that the golfer can adopt to combat it. You can measure a slope by eye and judge how much it will turn the putt. Looking at grain tells you only the direction your ball will be deflected, if at all. There is no visual indication of how severe that deflection might be. As a rule of thumb, it is nearly always safe to assume that in temperate climates, the grain will not move the ball far off line, and so you do not aim wide of the hole and trust the grain to swing the putt into the cup. Aim off slightly to the right or left of the center of the hole to allow for grain, but always keep the line inside the width of the hole so that if the putt does run straight, the ball will drop.

As for hotter climates, the only sensible advice is to rely on the procedures that have been stressed over and over in this book. Observe that the green is grainy. Observe the direction of the grain. Observe the way your own putts behave on the practice green. Observe other people's putts. Absorb as much information as you can about the way grain affects both the pace and the deflection of putts down grain, up grain, and across grain. Resist all temptations to hysteria and the negative conclusion that putting on such greens is a lottery. Reassure yourself that there *is* a way and that your superior intellect and approach to the problem will provide the answers. Do *not* attempt to work out a sliding scale of grain, telling yourself that a ten-foot putt will be deflected by three inches and a twenty-footer by four and three-quarter inches. Just absorb as many facts as you can and let your subconscious mind make its own calculations—always remembering, of course, that your subconscious mind cannot take grain into consideration if you have failed to notice its existence in the first place.

So much for natural variations on the putting surface. Unfortunately, there are other pitfalls for the unwary golfer. Public demand for greens of pool-table quality means that vast amounts of labor and material resources must be devoted to pampering those sacred swards of turf. This in turn means that club golfers frequently encounter greens that have just been verticut, or hollow-tined, or top-dressed, or even—on the "browns" of central Africa and the Middle East—given a light spraying with sump oil. The common reaction by many golfers when they see that such work has been done is to fall into a mood of fatalism and to complain: "How do they expect anyone to putt on greens in this condition?"

This response inevitably results in a casual, even despairing, approach to putting and, just as certainly, a marked lack of success followed by even more despair. Such a reaction is closely related to another phobia—fear and hatred of certain shots. Golfers talk about how they loathe playing from thick rough, or hitting long bunker shots, or tackling sloping lies, or extricating a ball plugged in sand, or driving in a left-to-right wind, or playing from divot holes, or chipping on Bermuda grass, or approaching elevated greens, or carrying cross bunkers, or hitting over water, or even how they just can't get interested in putting. The one thing that can be said with absolute certainty about a golfer with such a hang-up is that he is not a real player and will never be much good at the game. What is there to hate in golf, for goodness sake? If you have a prejudice against a particular shot or situation, the thing to do is to lose no time in eradicating the object of your disfavor. Forget about the weekly fourball for once and spend the day on the practice range working that hatred out of your system. Hit shots out of divot holes from morning to night, experimenting and taking such expert advice as you can muster, and continue working on that shot until you have mastered it. It does not take long to eliminate the poison of fear from the bloodstream. Once you are confidently

finding the bottom of the ball with a crisp, descending blow, move on to more advanced techniques until you can fade or draw your divot-hole shots with equal facility. There are few greater satisfactions in golf than acquiring a new skill, and there is a potent psychological bonus as well. Once you have eliminated divot shots from your hate list and have accepted them as a challenge to be relished with the sure anticipation of success, you will enjoy the comforting feeling of being one up on all your opponents who dislike divot-hole shots. You now have an edge, to the point perhaps of even looking forward to finding your ball in a divot as an opportunity to exercise your special talent. The same goes for putting in general, and putting on rough greens in particular. Just remember that no matter how blemished the putting surface may be, a good putt will have a much better chance of success than a casual or quit stroke.

Nearly every golfer has a favorite shot. Among high-handicappers it is often enough a short-iron from a level lie: it's commonplace for a twenty-four-handicap golfer to hit his eight- or nine-iron with almost the skill and assurance of a single-figure player. That being the case, it is more than likely that he could learn much to his advantage about his golf clubs, possibly getting an expert to match his set to the feel and balance of that favorite club. But an even greater reward awaits him if he matches his mind to that favorite shot. The aim should be to make every shot and every situation an equal favorite. Instead of shrinking from the need to hit a long-iron into a brisk headwind, the golfer must achieve the frame of mind that welcomes the chance to pull out his two-iron and clip a screamer under the wind straight at the target. The satisfaction of such a shot is well worth the labor of mastering its execution.

You have to love putting, as much if not more than belting that two-iron or a full drive. Putting is more than half the game, and it is pointless to regard it as a boring chore that has to be endured for the sake of the more satisfying pleasures of golf. The surest way to get to love putting is to become good at it, and one way to become proficient on all greens is to welcome the opportunity to play on bad greens. Your opponent may well have "one of those days" and fluke in a string of long putts when the greens are in pristine condition, but when the surfaces are covered with bungholes or top-dressing, it takes more than luck to overcome the problem. With your special talent and exceptional enjoyment of the challenge, you have the match in your pocket before you start. Accept things for what they are, rather than good or bad, or easy or difficult, or beautiful or ugly. It is damaging to put judgment values on bouncy fairways or soft greens. If the fairways are bouncy, adjust your game to suit the bounce and get on with enjoying the game. If the greens are soggy, simply resolve to pitch right up to the flag. Avoid preferences because, in golf, you do not get a choice, and since you have to play the course the way it happens to be, the prudent approach is to *like* it that way.

By the same token, it is self-defeating to think in terms of bad lies, unlucky bounces, and the malevolence of fate. You meet golfers who have developed persecution complexes, believing themselves to have been singled out for special attention by the vengeful gods of the game. You know what they say: "With my luck, that one will roll into the lake"; "I see I've got the mandatory rock behind my ball"; "These bunkers are a positive disgrace"; "Just look at the state of this fairway—the whole thing ought to be declared ground under repair." Such whiners and moaners are often the fastest guns in the West when it comes to whipping out the rule book and claiming free relief. The real golfer takes such situations in his stride. After all, he has exorcised his personal demons on the practice tee and has learned how to cope with tight lies because in his practice sessions he has deliberately stepped on his practice balls and pressed them into the turf, while all around him others were nudging each ball onto inviting tuffets.

The Rules of Golf are intended to provide relief in cases when it is impossible to play a shot through no fault of the golfer, and they clearly specify the conditions from which relief is available. It is true that the rules are not just a set of prohibitions; they are also the golfer's bill of rights, and on occasion they provide a distinct advantage. It is entirely within the spirit of golf to accept these bonuses, provided that you are equally meticulous about accepting the disadvantages. Take the example of a puddle on the edge of a fairway. A free drop from casual water is available at *the nearest* point that provides maximum relief from such a condition, and it is a matter of *measurement,* not length of grass, whether the drop is made onto the fairway or in the rough; not a question of good or bad luck, but just a case of impersonal, unemotional inches.

There is something to be said for the policy of treating such rules as a court of last resort and first examining whether it might not be preferable to play the ball as it lies. The pleasures of golf are enhanced if success is achieved without fortunate rubs of the green or the help of the rule book. But the main benefit of accepting things the way they are is, of course, that such an attitude makes you a better player. If you think right you are more than halfway to playing right—and never more so than on the green.

A continuing debate in golf, especially in the context of tournaments and championships, concerns the "proper" speed of greens and whether it is essential, or even desirable, for all eighteen to be uniform in speed and texture. The discussion gathered intensity back in 1978, when the United States Golf Association adopted a device originated by Edward S. Stimpson for measuring the speed of greens. Before then, we had to assess pace by human judgment, such as Sam Snead's remark that stopping the ball on a downhill putt was tougher than putting down a marble staircase. The Stimpmeter provided numerical values for green speeds.

The instrument itself has the elegance of simplicity; it is just a strip of grooved aluminum with a notch near one end. A ball is placed in the notch, and that end of the device is then carefully raised. At a predetermined angle the ball releases itself from its notch by natural inertia and rolls down the groove. Since that release angle is always the same, so the speed of the ball when it reaches the green is constant. The distance the ball rolls on the green is measured, and then the exercise is repeated in the opposite direction to provide a mean figure in case the green is not absolutely level. Normally, the operator will complete three rolls in each direction and then work out the average distance. A Stimpmeter reading of 4' 6" is rated slow; 5' 6" medium slow; 6' 6" medium; 7' 6" medium fast; and 8' 6" fast. Clubs such as Oakmont, which are known for the speed of their greens, achieve Stimpmeter readings in excess of 11, and the United States Golf Association likes to prepare Open championship greens, depending on the degree of contouring, at double-figure speeds.

Golf is divided into two schools of thought about the Stimpmeter. One side claims that it is a valuable tool for course superintendents in creating uniformity of speed on all greens and for locating fair cup positions. The other side represents the historical traditions of golf and abominates the introduction of such numerical analysis of a glory of nature.

The Royal and Ancient Golf Club of St. Andrews, for instance, does not possess a Stimpmeter and presently has no intention of acquiring one, probably on the grounds that the head greenkeeper would undoubtedly hurl it into the North Sea. We may assume that the reaction would be the same in the case of another device, nicknamed the "Mushmeter," for measuring the softness of greens, a task undertaken perfectly adequately for the best part of five centu-

*Me and my shadow, as the two minds of
Jerry Pate and Ben Crenshaw seek but a
single thought.*

OVERLEAF
*They also serve who only stand and
wait—Lance Ten Broeck with the
backing of venerable advice.*

ries by the prodding of a greenkeeper's sensitive thumb. The best advice is to maintain a lofty detachment from this unprofitable debate, although it may be difficult for a rational being not to recoil from the thought of standardized golf courses. One of the glories of the game is that, because every course is different, variety is the spice of golf, no less than of life.

Despite the obviousness of this fact, there is an insidious movement in golf toward standardization. This pernicious doctrine maintains that a course is in some way substandard unless it measures at least seven thousand yards off the back tees; has a par of seventy-two composed of matching halves of two par-threes, two par-fives, and five par-fours; its fairways of emerald green grass are trimmed to a uniform three-quarters of an inch; bunkers are furnished with dazzling white sand; the rough is cut precisely to four inches and separated from the fairways by a six-foot band of two-inch semirough; the water hazards have the appearance of Scandinavian blue crystal, even if this means poisoning the fish with dye; the landing areas for the drives are between twenty-five and thirty yards wide; and the greens are soft enough to hold a half-topped three-iron and clipped to three-thirty-seconds of an inch.

The annual worldwide exposure on television of Augusta National for the Masters Tournament has undoubtedly contributed to this unwitting ideal of what every golf course should be, but, gorgeous as Augusta is, it is a grotesque distortion of values to seek to reproduce it in the desert of Arizona or the coral islands of the Caribbean. Heaven forbid that we think in terms of "proper" golf courses or "proper" speeds for greens. And as for uniformity of speed for all eighteen greens, the critical factor must surely be that the golfer has the evidence available to judge the speed on *any* green, provided that he has the wit to read the signs. Thus there can be no serious objection to a green that is closely hemmed in by mighty trees being slower

than the other seventeen because the golfer has every opportunity to judge for himself that its shaded site will retain moisture longer than its fellows.

Anything in golf that encourages the player to think before he plays his shot, then rewards him for superior powers of observation and analysis, should be retained and encouraged. In the same way, any move that enables a mindless automaton to go around a standard golf course playing a succession of standard shots should be firmly resisted. Hitting the shots is the lesser part of the game.

The golfer is permitted to solicit advice from his caddie and his partners, and some modern tournament professionals have formed liaisons with regular caddies that come close to turning the game into a team contest. It is no extravagance to engage a caddie who unerringly reads the correct line of every putt; who selects the correct club for every occasion and counsels the correct type of shot to be played; who listens when you feel like talking and who holds his peace when you prefer silence; who elevates your spirits when you are downcast and who keeps you on an even emotional keel when things are going well; who meticulously maintains your equipment in prime condition; and who does not steal cigarettes from the glove pocket of your golf bag. The only problem is that such a creature has not been born.

This is not to say that caddies and partners cannot help. They can, provided that their advice passes a rigorous test of quality control. If you get to the first green and your caddie, or a partner, attends the flag and announces confidently: "The line is four inches outside the right lip," you should treat him and his advice with deep mistrust. Since he cannot know your putting style, whether you stroke your putts firmly or play them to die into the hole, the suggestion of a four-inch break is of no value and may well be misleading. The same goes for clubbing. You are the only person who knows how hard you propose

to hit the particular shot you have selected, so you, and you alone, must make all the decisions involving judgment.

Information, of course, is something else. By all means feed on the local knowledge of your caddie or of a partner, who knows the course. Remember, also, that the rules permit you to ask questions of fact from anyone, so you may legitimately inquire of an opponent—or a fellow competitor, or even a bystander—the length of a hole, or whether it dog-legs to the left or right, because this is information openly available to anyone. But you may *not* ask these people if, for instance, a four-iron will get you home because that is a question involving golfing judgment, and only the advice of your caddie or partner may be sought on such matters.

Once a caddie has convinced you that he has the measure of your putting technique and has correctly read the line for you a few times, a measure of reliance can be placed on his future advice. But even then, the buck stops with you. If you see the line as a right-lip putt, and he tells you that it will break the other way, you have a problem. If you take his word and miss the putt, you do not get to replay the stroke, and you also get no sympathy. So, when you have a conflict, you should always put your trust in your own judgment, thereby exonerating the caddie from all blame if you happen to miss and preserving a healthy relationship with him.

On the other hand, if you hole the putt, you will be so pleased with yourself that you will be in a forgiving mood. In fact, an astute caddie can occasionally perform a valuable service by deliberately contradicting your own first impression. If you are fairly but not completely sure that you have seen your line, and you need reassurance, the very act of discussing it with someone is often enough to confirm your selection. Human nature being what it is, we naturally harden our judgments when they are challenged, just as we are reinforced in our opinions when they receive outside support. The main thing is to be positive in your vision of the correct line and to accept total responsibility for your decision. What you must avoid at all costs is to allow yourself to become subordinate to someone else's judgments, so that in effect another person is playing the golf and you are simply hitting the shots by proxy. Be your own person, and if things go wrong, blame no one, not even yourself. You are human and therefore fallible. And if you are constantly in a state of self-reproach, you are hardly in condition for the dispassionate observation that will enable you to learn from your mistakes.

Finally, in the cause of enlightenment and amusement, let us hear some of the observations on putting made by people who have earned the right to speak with authority on the subject:

Willie Turness (U.S. Amateur champion 1938, 1948; British Amateur champion 1947): "Putting is easy."

Joyce Wethered, later Lady Heathcoat Amory (British Ladies' Open champion 1922, 1924, 1925, 1929): "A few golfers still remain, although I believe their numbers are diminishing, who like to make you believe that their nerves never trouble them. But one never quite knows if they are speaking the truth. If they are, one is tempted to exclaim, 'What a pity!' "

Tommy Armour (noted golf instructor who taught Babe Zaharias): "Those who think in terms of golf being a science have unfortunately tried to part from each other the arms, head, shoulders, body, hips, and legs. They turn the golfer into a worm cut into bits, with each part wriggling in every-which-way direction. I call it paralysis by analysis."

Max Faulkner (who was signing his autograph "Open champion, 1951" with two rounds still to play): "Four footers? I shall never miss another of those."

Henry Longhurst (British golf essayist, commenting on the above boast): "I moved silently away lest fate mistake me for an accomplice and in some way give me the hammer, too."

Ben Hogan (U.S. Open champion 1948, 1950, 1951, 1953; U.S. PGA champion

1946, 1948; Masters champion 1951, 1953; British Open champion 1953): "If the tees and fairways are in bad shape I'll play, but if the greens are lousy I don't start."

Harry Vardon (British Open champion 1896, 1898, 1899, 1903, 1911, 1914; U.S. Open champion 1900): "There are many ways of performing the operation successfully. I can claim, however, to be in a position to explain how not to putt. I think I know as well as anybody how not to do it."

Jack Nicklaus (U.S. Amateur champion 1959, 1961; U.S. Open champion 1962, 1967, 1972, 1980; British Open champion 1966, 1970, 1978; Masters champion 1963, 1965, 1966, 1972, 1975; U.S. PGA champion 1963, 1971, 1973, 1975, 1980): "The real reason for all my fidding around is that I really do believe that putting is inspiration, not mechanical."

Sandy Herd (British Open champion 1902), after being thoroughly outputted in a match by an amateur: "Look here, you wouldn't hole the putts you've been holing today if you had to do it for your living."

Doug Sanders (he of the short swing and colorful raiment): "Since no two greens are the same, practice and judgment based on experience will help you more than any instruction."

Walter Hagen (U.S. Open champion 1914, 1919; U.S. PGA champion 1921, 1924, 1927; British Open champion 1922, 1924, 1928, 1929): "Three of those and one of those count four. I always understood that."

James Braid (British Open champion 1901, 1905, 1906, 1908, 1910): "Very few golfers take any wind that may be blowing sufficiently into their consideration when putting."

Bruce Devlin (noted Australian professional): "It is the ability to hole putts consistently from six feet and less that counts most."

Willie Park, Jr. (British Open champion 1887, 1889): "The man who can putt is a match for anyone."

Gay Brewer (Masters Champion 1967): "If you can convince yourself the ball is going in the hole, you'll get it there often whatever kind of stroke you use."

George Duncan (British Open champion 1920): "If you are going to miss 'em, miss 'em quick."

The expert witnesses have had their say. You have also heard a great deal of testimony about the variable nature of the greens and the no less variable nature of golfers. You have been assailed by warnings and exhortations, and the time has arrived to summarize these proceedings and attempt to distill the essence of how to prepare yourself to putt.

The first advice is to dismiss, if you can, the notion that putting is a physical action that starts when you step up to the ball. Think of it rather as a state of mind that begins at the moment your ball lands on the green, or possibly on the fringe. The putter will often be the best club to use from off the green for, in the immortal words of the playing half of this authorship team, "Your worst putt will be as close as your best chip."

Having switched your mind into the putting mode, you should be eager, alert, and observant of all about you, noting the lie of the land and the weather conditions as you walk to the green and taking in closer detail as you reach your ball. Be dispassionate about what you see, ascribing neither virtue nor malice to the state of the green, the slope, the grain, or any other factors that may influence the behavior of your putt. Watch other putts in this same mood of objective detachment. Particularly, cultivate the habit of a set procedure for sizing up your putt. The form of that procedure is a matter for individual choice, and what follows is intended only as a guide, or specimen, to be adapted to your own preferences.

When it is your turn to play, observe your putt from behind the ball. Take another sighting from about six feet short of the hole. Inspect those last few feet with care, removing any loose impediments you think might deflect the ball. Look into the hole. Grass lying across the rim of the cup will reveal the direction of any grain. Besides, according to the psychologists, the close-up view of the hole will imprint on your mind the ample size of your target and give you confidence. As you return to your ball, make a detour, stopping halfway to observe your putt from the side. This will give you a different view of the upslopes and downslopes over which the ball must travel, and it will also reinforce your feelings about distance and speed. Finally, take another look from behind your ball, forming in your mind's eye a vision of the ball rolling along its predestined path and disappearing into the hole. Put all your trust in that vision, grasp your putter with the gentle touch you would use to lead a small child across the road, and consign the next few moments to the merciful custody of your subconscious self, as outlined in the next chapter.

FAITH–WITHOUT HOPE OR CHARITY

The more I practice, the luckier I get.
                                    – *Gary Player*

How do you peel an apple? You hold it in your left hand and wield the knife with the right. You do the same when cutting a steak. You steady the meat with the fork held in the left hand and slice with the knife in the right hand. You hold a book with the left hand and turn the pages with the right. You write a letter by using the left hand as a paperweight and write with the right hand. (That neglected band of left-handed golfers will not need reminding by now that they must transpose all these left-hand and right-hand references).

In all everyday actions calling for precision, the natural instinct is to employ the left hand in a passive role, if at all, and to use the dexterity of the master right hand to perform the intricate work. The only time we apply both hands in unison is when the job calls for the strength of both hands. In putting, it is never necessary to apply the combined force of both hands, and so logic suggests that the right hand should play the active part, perhaps even the *only* part.

This theory can be tested by a simple experiment. Take your putter into a bunker and find a level area of sand. Using a two-handed grip and moving the putter at a speed appropriate for a twenty-foot putt, scrape a straight line in the sand with the sole of the putter. Scratch the surface lightly, with just enough downward pressure to produce a visible impression in the sand of the path of your stroke. Now repeat the performance, but this time take the left hand completely off the putter. Remember, the object of the exercise is to draw as straight a line as possible. If your one-handed line proves to be markedly straighter, which will almost certainly be the case, you can safely conclude that you achieve greater control of the clubhead by wielding the putter with your master hand only.

Walter Travis, the father of scientific putting, came to the same conclusion:

> I believe that putting should be done always with one hand—with one hand actively at work, that is. The left hand should be used only for the purpose of swinging the clubhead backwards preparatory to taking the stroke. When it has done that its work is done, and the right hand should then be the sole master of the situation, the left being merely kept in attachment to it for steadying purposes. When only one hand is thus employed the gain in accuracy is very great. Two hands at work, on a short putt or a long one, tend to distraction. When the stroke is being made the grip of the right hand should be firm, but not tight, and after impact the clubhead should be allowed to pass clean through with an easy following stroke. The follow-through should indeed be as long as possible to make it comfortably and with this object in view, at the moment of touching the ball the grip of the fingers of the left hand should be considerably relaxed so that the right hand may go on doing its work without interruption.

Paul Runyan, another acute analyst of technique, also firmly believed in the doctrine of using the master hand to control the action. His solution was to use a putter with a shaft six inches longer than normal and to use a split-handed grip. The left hand held the club at the top of the grip and acted solely as a pivot. The right hand, placed well down the shaft with the palm facing the target, made the stroke.

The same one-handed principle inspired the croquet style of putting, with the player standing astride the target line and swinging the club between his legs. The ruling bodies banned croquet putting, and Sam Snead pioneered his sidewinder technique of facing the hole with the ball positioned just outside his right foot. He thus retained the advantages of split-handed putting and two-eyed sighting of his target without contravening the laws.

The question has often been asked, and with considerable emotional emphasis, why croquet putting was banned. After all, its main effect was to extend the golfing lives of players whose nerves had deteriorated to the point that they were incapable of putting in the conventional way. The United States Golf Association and the Royal and

Ancient Golf Club operate by the lofty principle of "Never complain, never apologize, and never explain," but we may safely assume that their motives could be summed up in the phrase: "It isn't golf." That would be a perfectly reasonable, even laudable, explanation because golf has always been a sideways game and not a head-on game. Their decision cannot have been simply because of an abhorrence of standing astride the line because that has always been permissible in golf and, indeed, still is with the sole exception of shots on the putting green. The reason must lie locked within the inscrutable portals of the rules of golf committees, but it is well nigh impossible for the simple layman to imagine an objection to croquet putting that does not apply with equal force to the sidewinder style. Maybe the legislators are just waiting for Sam Snead to retire before heaping another load of legal prohibitions onto the hapless heads of the golf populace.

A number of players have pursued the one-handed theory to its logical conclusion. The accomplished amateur Joe Turnesa won the Metropolitan Open putting one-handed. Others have used a tiny putter the size and shape of a tack-hammer, holding it with one hand only, of course. With this weird implement—and very effective it is on short putts—the authorities are on firmer ground for their disapproval, because Rule 4 says: "The club shall not be substantially different from the traditional and customary form and make." We may take issue with the lawgivers on semantic grounds for their overkill use of both "traditional" and "customary," and also of both "form" and "make," but all golfers must endorse the sentiments of that prolix rule. We all know what golf clubs are, and many of us have a natural if irrational resistance to odd-looking clubs. Good for us. That conformist instinct, however, can be destructive in golf. There must be thousands and thousands of golfers who would be happier and much more effective if they held the club for the full shots with a two-handed grip, but they persevere with a Vardon grip because that is the done thing. Likewise, there is considerable sales resistance in golf to split-handed putting styles because players think they look odd. Odd, indeed! There is nothing odd about rolling in thirty-footers. There is only one convention about putting styles worth a hoot, and that is the eternal truth: "The best method is the one that works best for you."

Experimentation is one of the joys of golf (at the right time and in the right place, of course), and the master-hand theory offers an obvious area for experiment. Desperation is often the slavedriver that sends the golfer to the practice green with a selection of clubs and a head full of theory. In such cases, the problem almost certainly has nothing to do with the player's stroke, thus the root cause of his troubles will continue to affect whatever fancy grip or method he may contrive. That is not to say that a change of putter cannot work wonders because it can. So can a change of grip or stance. But the improvement is temporary, and changes born of desperation are no more than palliatives. The cure for desperation may more likely be found in the consulting room of a marriage counselor, or a bank manager, or a sports psychiatrist. For this reason, we should be wary of dismissing unorthodox putting styles on the grounds that Bloggins uses such and such method and he can't putt for peanuts. Bloggins is almost certainly the victim of some disorder, the last person you would choose as the exponent of a putting action. But *you* are totally rational, superbly coordinated, relaxed, so packed with confidence that it is spurting from your ears in two fine jets, and enjoying a magical touch on the greens. Such is the appropriate condition for experimental work, and in *your* hands the Bloggins method could be devastatingly effective.

Another aspect of the master-hand theory may well be worth exploring. Which *is* your master hand? The answer may not be so obvious as it appears. Just because a man plays golf right-handed it does not follow that he is naturally right-handed. About one person in ten is naturally left-handed,

Stand in line with the ball and the hole, close one eye, and allow the putter to hang in a vertical plane aligned with the hole. If the ball is now on the left side of the putter shaft it means that the green slopes from left to right. Always remember that plumb-bobbing provides a rough guide, not an accurate measurement of the amount of swing on the putt. If the green has contra-opposed slopes the system may even be misleading, so treat the readings with a certain reserve. In fact, plumb-bobbing should always be treated as just one of the many factors in your reading of the line.

yet there is nothing like that proportion of left-handed golfers. Children who take up the game often start with any clubs that happen to be available, and in the vast majority of cases such cast-off clubs are right-handed. Indeed, some instructors who advocate left-side dominance in golf approve of left-handers playing right-handed. Even if that were sensible for the long game, however, it would not apply to the delicate precision of putting. Left-handedness is not, it seems, simply a reversal of the natural order. It appears that left-handers have distinct mental characteristics that give them a special aptitude for certain functions. To judge by the uncanny skills of the New Zealander Bob Charles, it could well be that putting is one of them.

The work of the Harvard neurologist the late Professor Norman Gerschwind certainly raises the possibility that the special talents required for putting have their origins in the right side of the brain, which controls the left hand. That would at least explain why right-handers putt poorly. On the face of it, the evidence that the left side of the brain is predominant in the right-handed golf swing is overwhelming, since fewer than 1 percent of the leading golfers play left-handed, compared with four out of ten among the best tennis players. But, though the putting stroke can be described as a golf stroke in miniature, it has the unique elements of delicacy and restraint, which could well be functions of the right side of the brain. In any case, it is obviously a wise precaution to check whether you have superior control and touch when putting left-handed. A number of tournament professionals, notably the Canadian Jim Nelford and the American Mac O'Grady, play right-handed but switch to the left for putting.

The purpose of this book is not to teach putting because putting cannot be taught. Putting is like wisdom, partly a natural gift and partly the accumulation of experience. That is a discouraging thought, you may protest. Surely there is *something* about putting that can be taught, if only the best

way to hold the club. Sorry, there is not a best way. There is also no right way to stand to the ball or correct method of swinging the club. The only dogmatic statement that can be made about putting is that no dogmatic statements can be made about putting.

There is an abundance of information that can be accumulated, from the properties of grass to the coefficient of restitution of the golf ball, but when the golfer stands over a putt no amount of knowledge is of the slightest use to him. Indeed, a case can be made for the proposition that ignorance is a more effective ally than knowledge to the putter. Who are the best putters in the world? Certainly not the tournament professionals. They are not in the same class as young children who do not even know how to hold the club. Often their grandmothers are pretty useful, too, even when putting with a pocketbook swinging from the wrist. The place to see putting of truly astonishing standard is on the greens of fairgrounds and amusement parks. And the reason children are so deadly is that no one has ever told them how difficult it is to putt, so, in their ignorance, they think it is easy. And so it *is*. There is nothing to it, and so there is nothing to teach. You cannot teach innocence; once that goes it is gone forever.

The best we can hope to do in this book is to stimulate interest and to explore some of the ways a golfer can seek his own salvation on the greens. And here again putting is like wisdom; the secret of both is that if you ask the right questions, the answers take care of themselves.

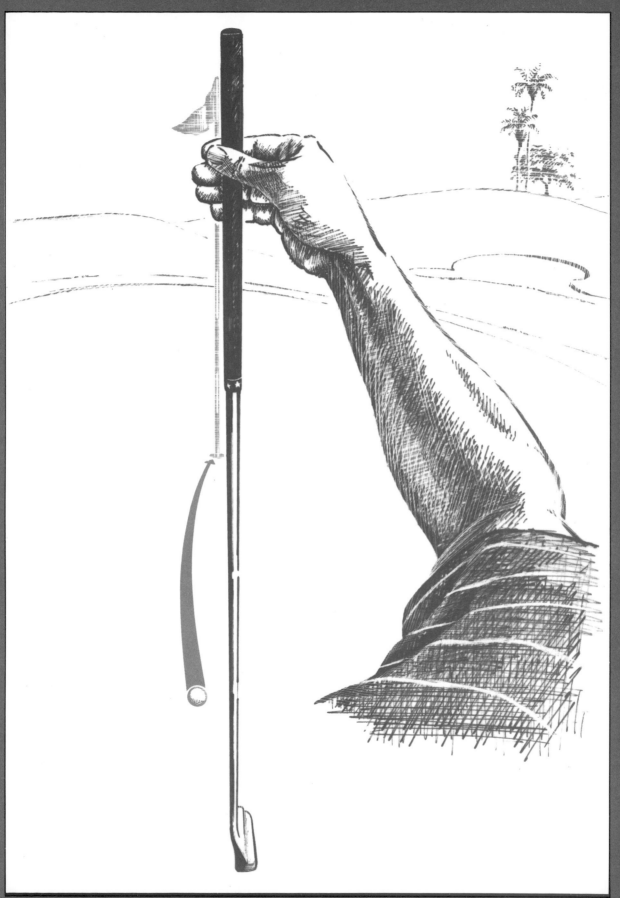

The first question a golfer must ask himself—and this applies to the whole sweep of golfing activity from strategy to stroke-making, not just to putting—is: What manner of person am I? If you watch the great players you can make accurate character assessments of them from the way they play. Julius Boros's languid swing reveals the man, relaxed and deliberate in everything he does. David Graham's purposeful march up the fairway and methodical, almost mechanical, action is a faithful expression of his decisive personality. Everything Jack Nicklaus does on the golf course mirrors the keen, analytical nature of the man. In other words, their golf is true to themselves, and that is how it always must be if progress is to be made in this game. Golfers love to shape their games on the model of their heroes, and that is fine provided that hero and student are fundamentally alike in personality and temperament. But there is no future in copying Lanny Wadkins's whizz-bang style if you happen to have the laid-back personality of Don January. So, unto thine own self be true. Then, having established the truth about yourself, you are in a position to make a sensible judgment about one of the basic putting dilemmas: to rap or to stroke.

This is a vital decision because many other considerations depend on the answer, such as the type and weight of the putter, how tightly to grip the club, and, above all, how to assess the putt.

The difference in the two strokes—the short, sharp tap with a curtailed follow-through as perfected by Gary Player, versus the flowing and measured action of the stroke putter as personified by Ben Crenshaw—is not all that important in itself. The ball cannot distinguish any difference. What makes the distinction so critical is that rap putters almost invariably charge their putts, seeking to make the ball smack against the back of the cup, whereas strokers normally prefer to put just enough momentum on the ball so that it will barely topple into the hole on its final roll. Obviously, circumstances modify the styles. The rap putter does not rap too distinctly when he has a downhill, crosshill putt on a slick green. Similarly, the gentle stroker gets a certain amount of rap into his putt when he is going uphill against the grain on a shaggy green. But there are these two distinct types, with the action matching the player's attitude of mind, and those golfers who are indistinct or ambivalent about rapping or stroking are always indecisive putters.

There is no point in seeking to adjudicate on which method is better because, for the reasons explained above, the question of selecting one method over the other does not arise. You are either a rap putter or a stroke putter according to your destiny. Fortunately, both styles have clear virtues, and this should be well understood because, if nature has cast you as a rap putter, you need to be convinced that rap putting is immeasurably superior to stroking—and vice versa, of course, for stroke putters.

The most eloquent witness for stroking putts with just enough speed for them to die into the hole was Bobby Jones, whose formidable record adds telling testimony to his theme that this method presents the golfer with a much larger target. The ball can topple into the front of the hole, into either side, or even, every once in a while if the player is due for a reward on account of his sober and upright life, it can catch the side of the hole, roll gently around the rim, and drop in at the back—or through the tradesmen's entrance, in the popular British expression. So the effective catchment area of the hole with this method is almost three balls-widths, which provides a considerable margin for error. On the other hand, it must be said that the slower a ball is rolling—and by definition the stroke putter's ball is exhausting its impetus as it runs up to the hole—the more it is susceptible to deflection by slope and irregularities in the putting surface, such as holes made by spiked shoes.

Toward the end of a busy day when there has been heavy traffic on the course, it is common to see a putt heading on perfect line for the target lurch sideways like a drunken sailor in the last foot or so of its travel and miss the hole comfortably. It is at such times that the golfer's character is tested, and a word on that subject at this time may be in order. You have to realize that, despite any personal misgivings to the contrary, you are not being singled out for special treatment by a malign fate. These things happen to everyone, quite impartially. Therefore, nobody is terribly interested in listening to your hard-luck story, or even your fruity language. By gentlemanly convention, your playing companions or opponents are required to murmur "Bad luck," and by that same convention you are enjoined to suppress your inner turbulence, to adopt an expression of amused insouciance, and to tap in the tiddler with some light banality such as "C'est la vie." That way, you earn the reputation as a true sportsman with ice water in your veins.

The rap putters score because the putt is traveling at a fair lick as it reaches the hole and is therefore much less likely to fall away from its target line. That line has to be true, of course, because the target is effectively only two balls wide. The margin for error is considerably reduced because, whereas the stroked putt will topple into the side of the hole, the rapped putt on that line will invariably jump over the edge of the hole. Most rap putters aim to putt the ball to a precise spot about eighteen inches behind and dead on line with the center of the hole. That point about selecting a precise spot is important because in any task of manual dexterity, the closer the objective is defined, the greater becomes the chance of success. So on short putts the good player does not hit the ball toward the hole, but rather picks out the exact spot on the rim where he wants to direct the putt. When golfers miss these short putts they are inclined to confess to a lapse in concentration, but a better expression would be sloppy thinking. In all probability, the miss occurred because of a failure to program the mind with precise instructions. The same goes for all golf shots. The player who blazes away with his driver with no clear objective, simply to move it out as far as possible somewhere on the short grass, is much more likely to find the tall stuff than the player who picks out a clear target area on the fairway and especially if that specific area is within range of his average drive rather than his Sunday Special.

Rap putters may find Walter Travis's advice helpful in making a crisp contact. Travis experimented with the well-known system of picking a point of aim just in front of his ball, but he went a step further by extending a line back through the ball to a point behind it, giving him a visual aid for the approach path of the putter head onto the ball. He imagined that a tack was lightly stuck into the back of the ball just at the point where he wished to make contact, and his stroke, therefore, was a sharp tap to drive that tack into the ball with the sweet spot of the putter. One of the few pieces of advice about putting which might be advanced with the force of a golfing axiom is that, regardless of putting style, short putts should be struck firmly with a positive stroke. The history of golf is punctuated with tragic cases of golfers who lost championships through infirmities of stroke on short putts. Such putts should not die into the hole but, rather, perform a racing dive over the front rim.

The objective in putting should be to hole out every time, regardless of distance. The stroke putter should be concerned to lay his putt right on the rim of the cup, the rap putter to find his target eighteen inches beyond the hole. One school of thought says that, on long putts, the prime objective should be to make absolutely sure of getting down in two and that speed is therefore paramount because, even if the line is a bit off, a putt laid up at dead weight will leave a tap-in of no more than a couple of feet either side of the hole. This theory further suggests that the golfer who thus limits his ambition will reduce the pressure on his nervous system because

This is a dilemma of metaphysics which every golfer must resolve for himself. Do you visualize the curving path of the putt to the hole and strive to direct your ball along that path? Or do you judge how the putt will break and then use that information to site a target point, or phantom hole, so as to give yourself the simpler (?) task of hitting a straight putt? You do not need to be a scientific genius to realize that, regardless of the mental approach, the actual action of putting will be identical in both cases. But it is important to settle on one system or the other, and the practice green is the place to discover whether you function by putting to the real hole or by converting all your data of slope, grain, and wind into a target for a straight putt.

he has set himself a relatively easy task and thereby, freer of tension, will make a better job of it. Frankly, this is a negative attitude and a sure recipe for missing the hole.

There are occasions in golf, in match-play more often than in stroke-play, when two putts will serve as well as one, and in those rare instances discretion may well be the better part of valor and the golfer is justified in putting defensively. In that case, it may be useful to see the cup as the center of an imaginary six-foot circle and to limit your aim to stopping the ball within that circle. But when every stroke counts, settle for nothing less than a wholehearted commitment to directing the ball dead into the hole. Resist those siren voices which suggest that a cozy lag putt will be less wearing on the nerves. Nervous tension is part of the human condition. Accept it as such. Welcome it. Press your breast against the sharp sword of fear and defy it to deflect you from your resolve. Now, when you hole your twenty-footer, you will have won a battle to savor like nectar. These are the true victories of sport, of much more importance than the result of a golf game. But, of course, the sporting victories are the product of those victories over self.

Having satisfied yourself that you have identified your master hand for putting and the style best suited to your temperament, you are now equipped to bring rational thought to the question of how to grip the putter. Since all your preliminary work has been de-voted to clearing your mind of preconceptions so as to reestablish the innocence of your natural self, the way your hands fall naturally on the club will probably be the best style for you. It is wise to remember that your body knows perfectly well how to putt and how to belt out a drive, if only you can allow it to perform these tasks without confusing it with a barrage of instructions about taking care not to leave the ball on the high side of the hole, not to be short, and not, for goodness sake, to send the ball skating past the hole. The only effect of such warnings is to confuse the mind's guidance system, a mechanism far more sensitive and effective than the most sophisticated computer, and to guarantee that the nervous impulses that operate the muscles will become distorted and the stroke mishit. Similarly, the mind knows perfectly well how to hold a putter, and if you can permit it to do so without interference, then so much the better. If the grip feels right, it *is* right. It may well be, however, that your mind is so full of images of other people's grips, or theories about what constitutes the "right" grip, that you have lost touch entirely with your instinct.

In that case, it may be useful to review the functions of the grip and to look at a few variations. There are three ways of wielding a putter: (1) You can make the arms and the putter into one solid entity and pivot from the shoulders, keeping the wrists absolutely inflexible. (2) You can, theoretically, immobilize the arms and simply hinge the wrists, although nobody does. (3) You can combine the above actions in what is genuinely a miniaturized version of the full golf swing, part shoulder pivot and part wrist hinge. Of course, it is possible to contrive other ways of moving the putter-head, as Leo Diegel pioneered with his unique style of splaying the elbows and using them as the hinges, and there is also a hip-slide style that we will explore later as a remedy for the yips. But for all practical purposes the choice is between the shoulder pivot and the combined shoulder-arm-wrist action.

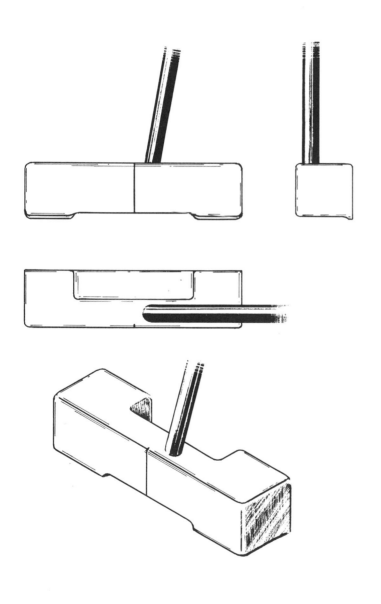

In the first case, the stroke is controlled by a push with the right hand, and the important thing is never to allow the left wrist to collapse. For this reason many golfers favor the reverse-overlap grip, that is, with all the fingers of the right hand holding the club and the index finger of the left hand overlapping the little finger of the right hand. The stroke is then firmly in the control of the master right hand. The reverse-overlap is also commonly used for the combination stroke, but, since this method is essentially a toned-down version of the golf swing, it obviously makes sense to retain your normal full-swing grip for putting. After all, you have invested an immense amount of time and experience in educating your hands to control a golf club with your big-game grip, so why confuse the issue by changing the grip to perform an identical function with the putter?

The first time they pick up a club, small children often position the left hand below the right. A few persevere with this curious method and become proficient at golf. The Indian golfer Sewsunker Sewgolum won several tournaments in Europe gripping left-below-right for all shots, and, though it cannot be recommended as a viable alternative to orthodoxy for the full swing, the fact that a dozen or more U.S. Tour players are using it on the greens indicates that it has definite merit as a putting grip.

One variation on conventional grips that has proved to be extremely efficacious is the "Over-Forties Finger," so called because of its reputed assistance for those whose nerves are reaching the end of their shelf life. The effect of pushing the right index finger straight down the shaft helps directional control, possibly because of the body's programming to extend a finger for purposes of tracing a straight line.

Most top players and instructors insist that, whatever the grip, the palms should be opposed, with the back of the left hand and the the palm of the right hand directly facing the target. That is a sensible arrangement if there is to be a hinging action in the stroke so that the wrists can operate in unison, just as it makes sense to line up the hinges on a door. But with a shoulder-pivot style, in which there is no breaking of the wrists, it is permissible to rotate that left hand either over or under the shaft, and, indeed, this may even be advisable if the golfer is having problems with a collapsing left wrist.

As to the contentious subject of how firmly to grip the putter, it is impossible to be dogmatic and equally impossible to put into words the feeling of an effective tension. The best we can do is to examine the function of grip pressure and to draw some general conclusions. The first thing to remember is that the tighter the grip, the greater the loss of delicate control: just try threading a needle when you are gripping with all your might. Nevertheless, the weight of the putter has to be supported securely and, particularly for rap putters, this requires a firm tension. Less pressure is advisable for stroke putters who use wrist action, and in both cases the master hand should be dominant in grip pressure as in everything else. It may sound like a cop-out, but the best advice is to grip the putter as lightly as you can while maintaining total control of the club.

In any case, grip pressure is just one element in the total package of putting, and once you have put everything together and achieved that state of grace in which you look at a putt and *know* that the ball is going into the hole, then details such as grip pressure are totally irrelevant. It happens all too rarely, but it does happen, that a golfer achieves this blessed state and holes everything. Ask him afterward how he held the club, or how tightly, or where he put his feet or the ball in relation to them, and he is as incapable of telling you as he would be of describing the movements of his hands when he ate his breakfast. The purpose of this book is to help golfers achieve that state in which they perform without knowing or giving the slightest thought to how they perform.

One practical tip is worth bearing in mind. When the state of play sets the pulse racing with excitement, it is a sound policy to make an objective assessment of your heightened tension and to recognize that your body will automatically respond to your nervous condition. In those cases, you should remind yourself as you walk between shots of the three remedies for tension: grip lightly, swing slowly, and make sure to complete the backswing.

Before moving on from the subject of the grip, we might as well dispose of the question of removing the left-hand glove for putting. The idea is that the bare hand benefits from the absence of that layer of leather which insulates the sensitive nerve endings. Actually, as we have seen, the function of the left hand for most people, regardless of style, is mainly that of a passenger, and it is in the master right hand that maximum sensitivity is required. Removing the glove may have some psychological benefit, in that the golfer feels that he has given himself the best possible chance of holing his putt by leaving nothing to chance in his preparations. But, to be honest, it is mainly a matter of habit. If there really were a distinct practical advantage in taking off the glove, golfers would do so before playing a little chip from the fringe. Also, as numerous Tour players past and present prove, it is possible to play excellent golf without wearing a glove at all, and in that case, of course, the dilemma does not arise.

Although the art of putting falls mainly into the domain of the sports psychologist, with the application of intangibles such as instinct and judgment, mechanical science does supply one imperative, in the identification and value of the putter's sweet spot. This is the point of balance and, as such, it really is a *point,* which means that you can safely ignore all those extravagant claims about certain clubs having "wide" sweet spots. The scientists tell us that it is vital to strike every putt on the sweet spot because only by so doing is it possible to achieve consistent weight of hit with every putt. If you contact the ball on either side of the sweet spot you will lose some of the momentum of the stroke and, in extreme cases, a loss of directional control as well.

You can ascertain the site of the sweet spot very easily. Hold the shaft of the putter very lightly in the left hand down near the head, with the face looking skyward and parallel to the ground. Now hold a golf ball about six inches above the face and drop it so that it bounces near the toe. You will distinctly feel the club twist at impact, and there will be a dead feeling from the bounce. Repeat the experiment, moving the point of impact along the face toward the center of the blade. There will come a point where the putter head remains in perfect equilibrium and the bounce feels lively. That is the sweet spot, and its position should be carefully noted, and even marked if you feel this will help. So, although the face of the putter may be more than four inches long (many putters measure exactly four and a quarter inches to match the diameter of the hole, but putters are available with faces as long as seven inches), its most effective striking area is about the size of a shirt button.

It follows, therefore, that contact between clubhead and ball is a matter of extreme precision, and this, in turn, has important implications for the way we should stand to the putt. Consider the way a portrait artist operates. When he is blocking in large areas of pigment he stands well back from his easel with arm outstretched, making bravura strokes with his brush and surveying the entire composition on his canvas. Then, as he gets to the detailed work, he moves closer, while grasping his brush more lightly. The key to this instinctive change in technique is eyesight. The finer the work, the more closely the artist needs to focus on the detail. A set of golf clubs is designed to serve the same purpose. The shafts become shorter as the function of the clubs changes from distance to accuracy, drawing the eyes closer and closer to the ball. The thirty-five-inch putter is thus the shortest club because it has the highest requirement for accurate contact. Now, if we understand that it is a matter of prime importance to make contact with the sweet spot, individual preference will dictate how low to crouch over the putt.

The eye is a vital source of the information from which the central nervous system will control the physical function of putting, and the eye must be given absolute priority in dictating putting style. Your eyes will tell you how close they want to be to the ball to ensure contact with the sweet spot, thus most of the questions about your stance should be settled for you instinctively by your vision. Some of the greatest putters in the world have bent double over their putts with their heads at about waist height, while others have stood almost as erect as soldiers undergoing inspection. Whatever your eyes want is what you should do.

Almost every instructional book stresses the importance of keeping the head still during the stroke, but that is to confuse cause with effect. Concentrate on delivering the sweet spot to the ball and your head will remain still as a natural consequence. Golf instruction is bedeviled by similar failures to distinguish cause from effect, by trying to cure measles by bleaching out the spots rather than diagnosing the disease and tackling its root cause. So get your eyes into the optimal position and let your body accommodate itself to that arrangement, in as comfortable and stable a position you can contrive.

If it does not make any difference to your ability to achieve pure contact whether you crouch or stand erect, there is one advantage of an upright posture that is not generally exploited. Eyesight again is the key. Peripheral vision is a variable facility, but people with normal sight are aware of objects in an arc of about forty-five degrees either side of their line of focus. On putts of more than about four feet, peripheral vision is valueless and the golfer must rely on his preliminary calculations and the set of his putter to control the direction of his putt. But on the short ones, peripheral vision can be very useful, especially if the golfer adjusts his stance to optimize the effect. It is certainly worth the experiment of

The golf swing—and a putt is a miniaturized swing—rotates around a point of pivot located in the region of the lower neck, here represented by Arnold Palmer impaled on a gigantic nail. The purpose of these gruesome images is to illustrate how the natural path of the clubhead varies with the posture of the player at the address position. With a relatively upright stance, the pivotal nail is necessarily inclined and the path of the clubhead follows an arc, curving inwards on the backswing, returning square to the ball, and then curving inwards again on the follow-through.

But when the player crouches well over the ball, the pivot is almost vertical and the clubhead can follow the path of a pure pendulum, straight back from the ball and straight through it again.

The lesson of these illustrations is that the player should set himself comfortably to the ball and then let that posture dictate how he swings the club. Any attempt to cross-fertilize these two elements, such as seeking to swing the club on a straight pendulum path from an upright stance, is a highly unnatural action and therefore very difficult to control.

taking up a stance with the ball positioned opposite or even outside the left foot and the head positioned as far as comfortably possible to the right, à la Jack Nicklaus. You now have an oblique view of the ball instead of the more usual eyes-over-ball arrangement and, while focusing on the ball, you are clearly aware of the hole in your peripheral vision. The putt now looks easy, and it *is* easy provided that its sheer simplicity does not induce carelessness in making a solid stroke. It should be added that peripheral putting does not carry the Arnold Palmer seal of approval because of the danger of taking the eye off the ball.

Having settled what manner of person you are, what style of putter you should be, how best to hold the club, and how to stand to the putt, we must now confront that dangerous and confusing subject of the actual stroke. Once again, provided that you have recaptured that glorious innocence of youth, you will not need to be told, nor to wonder, the line along which to swing the club during the backswing. But more likely, you will have read expert testimony from a dozen witnesses all revealing the secret (and secret it may well be in each individual case). The problem is that every secret is different, and, in golf as in so many other walks of life, what works for one person may well be disastrous for another. The first thing to do is to forget everything you have ever read or heard or observed on this subject and, thus deprogammed, to approach it in an open-minded spirit of scientific inquiry.

It all comes down to basic geometry. If you favor an upright stance and a shoulder-pivot style with the ball well in front of you, the geometry of this arrangement suggests that the clubhead should be moved in an arc in the manner of a full golf swing, that is, swinging inside the target line going back, returning momentarily square at the ball, then swinging back inside the line again on the follow-through. It *is* possible from this setup to take the clubhead straight back along the target line and return it on that same line, but physiologically that is an extraordinarily complex

and unnatural action and thus cannot be recommended as a consistent method.

From the above extreme there are infinite variations according to the relationship between the posture, the hands, and the ball, until we get to the other extreme, with both eyes and hands in a vertical line directly over the ball. From this position the natural movement is a pure pendulum stroke, to and fro along the target line. In short, the shape of the stroke should be adjusted to the method of the putt. For the pure pendulum style, the face of the putter should ideally be set at right angles to the shaft, as we can easily see. Unfortunately, the rules of golf insist that the clubhead must be offset by at least ten degrees from that desirable right angle, although in practice this is not a serious hindrance in pendulum putting.

Golfers often speak of getting a good roll on the putt, and they expend endless hours on the practice green to this end. Alas, they are chasing after a false god because it is impossible on any putt truly to roll the ball all the way to the hole. Many people find it impossible to accept that statement on trust, but it is very simply demonstrated by a quick experiment.

Lightly dust a path along a green with French chalk or some equally nontoxic power, then putt on that dusted surface. A twenty-footer will clearly illustrate how all putts behave. For about 20 percent of its travel the ball will actually be airborne, skidding above the grass with some backspin before skipping two or three times and then settling into an unbroken roll. During the rolling phase, the ball rides on top of the blades of grass, and as it loses its forward momentum, it settles down onto the solid surface of the green, all of which will be clearly discernible in the dusty turf (you can observe the same pattern when putting on greens from which the early morning dew has not been swept). It makes no difference to this pattern whether you strike the ball on the upswing or the downswing, or even if you deliberately make contact high on the ball with a half-topping stroke in an attempt to get it rolling smoothly right from the start. There is no point in trying to buck the laws of dynamics. But that is not to say that there is no point in practicing putting. Your intention should be to practice the important elements of grooving a smooth, repeating stroke that delivers the sweet spot surely to the ball time and time again.

The final element to be introduced into the integrated package of putting is a club to complement the holy alliance of temperament, physique, and style. Under the rules of golf the putter is the one club that may have the shaft fitted to any part of the head, and so the putter offers great flexibility to the designer. Similarly, putter grips do not have to be circular in section, and thus there is a wide range of grips shaped to help the golfer keep the face square to the line of putt.

Thus you have a rich array of shapes and sizes and weights and styles of putter from which to make a selection. Where should you start? Surely there must be sound scientific principles to be employed in narrowing down the choice, or at least in drawing up precise specifications for an implement that will be compatible with your individual style. There are indeed. The stance will dictate the correct angle of the lie of the clubhead and the length of shaft. Similarly, rap putters will normally feel happier with a light club, and stroke putters may find a heavier clubhead easier to control.

Unfortunately, there are powerful forces at work that render all such considerations seemingly irrelevant. Observe the Japanese player Isao Aoki, one of the most devastating putters in the professional game. Taking the logical approach, you would conclude that his putter is in urgent need of adjustment. The lie of the clubhead is all wrong because the toe at address is cocked high in the air. Aoki also grips the club well down the shaft, proof that it is too long for him. By all rational standards it is a most unsuitable club for Aoki. Yet by results—which must be the ultimate test—his putter is perfect for him.

What Aoki and others prove is that when it comes to choosing a putter we are entering into mysterious regions of the psyche and are at the mercy of subliminal prejudices. Thus, no matter how much it may offend against irrefutable scientific principles, we are forced to accept that the best way to select a putter is simply to fall in love with one. It sounds corny, and it *is* corny. But the heart is a much more vital organ than the brain in forming this partnership, which we hope will endure in perfect harmony till death do us part.

As with falling in love, the initial attraction is a matter of appearance. By golly, you think, but that is a gorgeous-looking putter, a real doll. The analogy must not be pushed too far for fear of indelicacy, but the next step is to get your hands on the object of your attraction. Pick up the putter and heft it in the hands, testing the weight and feeling the balance. Sometimes the rapport is immediate, and you know with a certainty which passeth all understanding that you were made for each other. There is nothing else for it but for you to possess this putter, regardless of cost and even if it means descending into larceny.

Among tournament professionals the incidence of theft of putters is shamefully high, although the dirty deed is always done with the compliance of the victim. If a fellow pro picks up your putter and insists that he must have it, the honorable traditions of this noble game demand that you do not stand in the way of his future happiness. It might be thought that an easier solution would be for the incipient thief to take a note of the brand and go buy one for himself. After all, putters are mass-produced these days, so two putters off the same production line must be identical. In fact, they are not identical at all, and not by a long way, even though the most sensitive scientific instruments are unable to detect any difference in weight, balance, or dimensions. Every putter has an indefinable feel, and it is not unusual for a tournament pro to go to the factory and heft a hundred or more seemingly identical weapons before settling on his choice. So it is a fortunate golfer who clicks right off the bat with the sultry-looking beauty that caught his eye in the shop. She (putters are always female) looks right and feels right. And now comes the moment of truth on the green where the lasting union may or may not be consummated.

Most golfers, it must be said, have to play the field before finding the perfect partner, and, as in all relationships, there is no guarantee of unbroken bliss. Lovers' tiffs are no less a part of the golf-putter partnership than they are of marriage, but, by the same token, patience and perseverance can restore harmony. And there is a sound practical reason for adopting this sentimental approach to the choice of a putter. If you can personalize your alliance with that insensate piece of metal, thinking of "her" rather than "it," as a faithful and trusty friend, as an ally that will give active assistance in holing putts, then you will have made a significant addition to the most precious commodity a golfer can command: confidence. Oscar Wilde defined faith as an unshakable belief in something you know to be untrue. Well, you know it to be untrue that a putter can respond to love, but it is immensely valuable if you can bring yourself to entertain an unshakable belief to the contrary because faith not only shifts mountains: it is the stuff that holes putts. John Low well understood the care and guile needed for the acquisition of a putter to be cherished and, though times have changed since 1903, the spirit of his delightful essay "How to Go about Buying a Putter" is as valid as ever:

If you wish a good putter, you will hardly expect to find one in a clubmaker's ready-made stock, far less in a toy shop or a tobacconist's window. The putter must be sought for with care and not hastily, for she is to be the friend, be it hoped, of many years. First, then, find out a workman of repute as a maker of putters—and in these days of "reach-me-down" clubs there are few such artists—and, having found him, proceed warily. It will never do to go and order him to make you a first-class club for your match next morning; you would probably receive only the work

of an apprentice. Wait your time and you will find the great man about his shop, or on his doorstep at the dinner hour, and may remark to him that the day is fine; this will be a safe opening, even though rain be falling in torrents, for it will give him the idea that you are a simple fellow and so throw him off his guard.

If a half-empty pipe lies beside him, offer him a cigar, and mention that you are afraid that it is not as good as you would have wished, being the last of the box, at the same time giving him to understand that another box is expected that evening. The cigar having been accepted and lighted, you may, in course of conversation, allude to a very fine putter made by a rival clubmaker which, you will tell your friend, is being much talked about and copied. This will be almost certainly a winning card to play, for there is much jealousy among the profession, and as likely as not the remark will be made that So-and-so—naming the rival maker—has about as much idea of fashioning a putter as he has of successfully solving the problem of aerial navigation. Do not press the matter to a conclusion, but meet your man again in similar manner, this time carelessly holding in your hand the club which you have long felt was the cause of the success of some distinguished player. Almost seem to hide it from the clubmaker, and he will be sure to ask to see it, and probably volunteer to make you one on the same lines with slight improvements of his own. In time you will get your putter, and it will probably be a good one. In any case it will be good enough to resell if it does not suit you, which is always a point to be considered.

There are three main tribes of putter—the blades, the mallets, and the center-shafted—and within each tribe are contained a multitude of variations. One very important property of a putter is that its shape should give you every help in setting it absolutely square to your chosen target line. It is the set of the putter that guides the line of the stroke. You have settled on your target line and you must set the putter at right angles to it. From that moment on there is no point in looking at the target except as a refresher to check your intended *speed* of putt. The putt is already aimed and locked on target. Many players advocate picking a spot, or even two spots, in front of the ball on the target line and then concentrating on putting over that spot. Jack Nicklaus is an advocate of this method, and he is one of the most formidable putters in the history of golf. Even so, the face of the putter must be square to the intended starting line of the putt because an error of one degree will mean a deviation of one and a half inches on a six-foot putt, enough to make the difference between a hit or a miss. The talent for seeing small deviations of angles is highly individual. Some people can detect it if a picture on the wall is one degree out of true. Small discrepancies are more difficult to spot within the relatively short span of a putter's head. Willie Park, Jr., understood the problem, and he was the first to advocate a long blade to help in squaring the face. Lines on the head of the putter may help, as with the popular Zebra model.

Although the intention should be to succeed with every putt, regardless of length, it should be recognized that the nature of the task changes with variations in distance. From a range of forty feet a good putter might expect, on average, to hole out once in about fifteen to twenty attempts. By improving his mental approach and his technique he could reduce those odds, but even so it would remain the exception rather than the rule for him to hole out from that distance. And though it is right and proper to believe that every putt is going to hit the dead center of the cup, it is nevertheless important for the golfer to keep the reality of his situation in mind. In this case, the reality is that he will probably need another putt, and therefore it is important that the second putt be a formality, a true tap-in. If that reality is totally discounted, the golfer might well charge too boldly for the hole and leave the ball too far beyond the hole to be sure of making the second putt.

That is not negative thinking. It would be negative thinking to tell yourself that you must not three-putt at any cost. The positive approach is to believe that the first putt will find its target but to accept that a spike mark could foil your perfect putt, in which case you will have an easy tap-in. It is therefore a matter of common sense that the critical factor in your forty-footer is *speed.* Above all, you must give enough weight to the putt to leave the ball within no more than three feet of the hole.

From six feet, however, the considerations are completely changed. At that range you do not have to concern yourself with pace because your instincts can handle that simple problem without conscious help. Anybody can instinctively judge the speed of a six-footer, thus the risk of overhitting the putt to such a degree as to create a crisis on the return is so slight as to be not worth considering. In this case the crucial factor is *line.* You have to concentrate your full attention on getting the direction absolutely right, and this in turn means a precise squaring of the putter face at the address.

Since we are concerned with two different functions, even though the differences are matters of degree, there could well be a case for employing two different implements. Everyone knows golfers who have a sure talent for hitting long putts close to the hole but are hopeless from close range, and vice versa. There is nothing to stop a golfer carrying two putters, provided he does not exceed the maximum permitted total of fourteen clubs in the bag. Here we run into the herd instinct of wishing to conform to the behavior of the majority. What would people think if you broke with convention and used two putters? What they might think and say will certainly undergo a rapid transformation if your tactics are successful. In that case, you may be sure that others will very quickly follow your example.

On the pro tours it is common to hear a player complain that he must change his putter because, though he can lay his putts

The hip-shimmy, or body putt. Sufferers from that dire malady known as the yips, or twitch, may well find relief on those nervy four-footers by adopting this style. It works on the principle that twitching is caused by a loss of control of the small muscles of the hands and wrists, so they must be immobilized. The arms are kept clamped firmly to the sides and the hands and wrists are similarly held rigid. From this position the only way to move the club is to slide the hips slightly to the right and then to slide them back, bringing the clubhead through the ball. It is not a particularly elegant style but it is effective, and the theory is that once the victim masters this method of holing-out he will lose his fear of short putts and his tendency to twitch will subside, allowing him to revert to his usual method. Unlike side-saddle putting (see Sam Snead, Chapter 5), another remedy for the twitch, the hip-shimmy is not recommended for long putts. That is not a matter of serious concern because most twitchers have no problems with the fuller swing of long putts.

dead from long range with it, he cannot sink the short ones. It is illogical in such cases for the player to discard a club that suits him perfectly for such an important function of the game. The sensible solution would be to supplement that club with a specialist putter for holing out. After all, a pro would not change a sand-wedge with which he performed miracles on bunker shots on the grounds that it did not suit him for playing running chip shots from the fringe but would automatically look for a supplementary wedge.

Perhaps to some extent we are inhibited by the language of golf. We speak of a putt for *any* stroke on the green and automatically associate that function with *the* putter. We do not make that same connection between the driver and the teeing ground because we habitually talk of the tee shot and make a club selection to suit the situation. Perhaps if tees had been called driving-grounds we would today have the same hang-ups about using any club but the driver to put the ball in play. All we are doing on the green is *playing golf shots,* and we should treat them as such, deliberately selecting the club for the task at hand rather than switching on the automatic pilot and letting reflex responses guide our

actions. So, if you should be fortunate to find putters that work superbly in their separate ways, one for holing out and the other for laying the ball dead from long range, you have a positive duty to yourself to carry them both. The laughter and the snide remarks will very quickly give way to envious congratulations.

You may possibly protest that the need to make room for a second putter will destroy your set. Let us be absolutely clear on this subject: there is no such thing as a full set of golf clubs. For 90 percent of golfers it is not only unnecessary to carry fourteen clubs but positively harmful because it suggests that there is a club for every shot. There isn't. Improvisation is the very soul of golf, and most golfers would become far better players—and get far more enjoyment from the game—if they carried fewer than fourteen clubs.

Possibly because putting is so much a mental and psychological function, little serious scientific research has been devoted to the subject. Nevertheless, since the rewards for improved performance are potentially so great, we should explore every aspect of putting. Perhaps science has a contribution to make to art. Certainly we should be prepared to listen closely when a scientist tells golfers that they are on the wrong track.

The late Dr. David Williams was a keen golfer, as well as a senior member of the team that designed the Concorde aircraft. He was responsible for the most thorough mathematical analysis of the golf swing ever undertaken, and he also applied himself to the problem of putting as a purely mechanical exercise. His starting point was the twin requirements of lining up the clubface square to the line of putt, then keeping the clubhead on that line during the stroke. To line up the clubface, golfers habitually stand at the address position and aim the club by turning the head to observe the target, then change focus from this sideways glance to adjust the set of the clubhead on the turf. That routine, claimed Dr. Williams, was scientifically unsound.

Far better to stand behind the ball with the eyes, club, and target in a direct line so that adjustments can be made with slight movements of the eyes. From experiments with a croquet-type putter he satisfied himself that such an arrangement does, indeed, make it easier to square the face accurately. He then designed a putter-head with features to facilitate the sighting process by this method. Now the golfer could be absolutely positive that his club was aiming on target, and he could concentrate exclusively on swinging the putter-head along that present line.

Dr. Williams well understood how nervous tension could affect the stroke, and he further argued that since the small muscles of the body are the ones most afflicted by nerves, finger tremor, and chattering teeth, it made sense to use only the large muscles for putts. We are talking of short putts, of course, because only when we get near to the hole do we experience difficulty in controlling the delicate muscles (which is why it is so rare for a golfer to suffer significantly with muscular control on long putts). The method Dr. Williams suggested was to grip the putter firmly and clamp the arms against the sides, turning club and entire upper body into one solid entity and thereby entirely eliminating the small muscles of the hands, arms, and shoulders. The ball is addressed opposite the left heel, with most of the body weight concentrated on the left foot. The stroke, kept as short as possible, is made entirely by a lateral slide of the hips, using only those big muscles of the legs not susceptible to loss of nervous control. This is a radical departure from conventional golfing practice, but the acid question is whether it works in practice. Oddly enough, no putter manufacturer has ever produced a commercial model of Dr. Williams's design, but at least we can all try that unorthodox putting method for ourselves, using any putter. It certainly offends against all received wisdom about gripping more lightly to counter the natural effects of nervous tension, but, of course, that applies to the orthodox arm-and-wrist stroke. Once again, the advice must be to examine this suggestion with an open mind and put it to the test.

A good putter averages a success rate of 55 percent on level six-foot putts, compared with 98 percent by a well-engineered putting machine, so there you have an objective standard against which to make your experiment. If you can achieve a significant improvement on that 55 percent rate with a hip-shimmy putting action, by all means adopt it. And you may cut your scores by employing both a separate putter and a separate putting style on the short ones.

One assertion can be made without fear of contradiction. For sufferers from the yips, or twitch, the hip-shimmy style offers by far the best hope for salvation. Yipping is a nervous affliction, and one by no means confined to golfers; it is part of a group of occupational disorders including scrivener's palsy (or writer's cramp), and among its victims are violinists, telegraphists, and milkers.

Tommy Armour was a sufferer, and he described the experience vividly: "That ghastly time when, with the first movement of the putter, the golfer blacks out, loses sight of the ball and hasn't the remotest idea of what to do with the putter, or, occasionally, that he is holding a putter at all." Harry Vardon, who once lost a U.S. Open championship because of missing a *one-inch* putt, put it this way: "As I stood addressing the ball I would watch for my right hand to jump. At the end of two seconds I would not be looking at the ball at all. My gaze would have become riveted on my right hand. I simply could not resist the desire to see what it was going to do. Directly, as I felt that it was about to jump, I would snatch at the ball in a desperate effort to play the shot before the involuntary movement would take effect. Up would go my head and body with a start and off would go the ball, anywhere but on the proper line." The yips have done for many another good golfer, notably Wild Bill Mehlhorn—who was finished after he jerked a three-footer clear across the green into a bunker—

Craig Wood, and, most excruciatingly, Ben Hogan.

It is well established that the yips affect the small muscles we employ for delicate work. One remedy, therefore, is to take the small muscles of the hands and arms out of the game and resort to the hip-shimmy method. Once the golfer has regained a controlled putting stroke, his nervous hysteria—which is always the root cause of the problem—may well subside and he can revert to his old putting style.

Since the nerves are the culprit, there is yet another way, brilliantly exploited by Sam Snead, and that is radically to change the nature of the putting action. Snead's solution was to modify croquet putting to make it conform with the rules and to adopt what he calls his "sidewinder" method. This method of Snead's avoids the disassociation between eye and hand because he has the target in binocular vision and thus aims his putt in a manner conforming with his natural instincts. The nervous system is much more familiar with this arrangement, as compared with the unnatural arrangement of looking in one direction and trying to direct the ball in another. Many golfers who adopt this style find that the yips are banished. Indeed, this is what Leonard Crawley, the British writer and Walker Cup player, had to say about sidewinder putting in Britain's *Golfing* magazine in 1957:

> About a year ago I went to Milan to play in the Italian Open Championship at Monza. I had played no competitive or even week-end golf all summer and was delighted to be hitting the ball respectably when I got to Italy. It was not until I began to go through the normal motions to strike my first putt that I realized I had "got 'em" at last. For years I had heard of "so-and-so" getting the jitters on the putting green but frankly never believed that this was more than a term of affection describing some rank bad putting. I felt completely paralysed and, in the course of the most appalling round of 85 shots, I took forty-six putts. Being a confirmed optimist where games are concerned I was convinced that it was due to a bilious condition and that it would never happen again. But, in the second round, my putting was even worse and so was my temper. I decided to give up golf and let it become just a pleasant memory of the past.
>
> Then one day I ran into my friend Selway, the Chairman of the [Royal and Ancient] Championship Committee, who said he had been suffering from the jitters for twenty years and that his whole golfing life had been ruined by them. He had now found the cure and I must try it. The croquet stroke was the one. He now reckoned to be dead from six feet.
>
> My own golf season ends in April and so I take up the story again in Italy, this time at glorious Villa d'Este two weeks ago. Once again I had my two "free of tension" rounds in the Italian Open, but this time with my croquet putter I was sublimely confident on the difficult slopes of those lovely greens. My opponent rather scoffingly observed, "You don't mean to say you use that thing, do you?" "Yes," I replied, "I am absolutely deadly with it." This was a pretty bold statement at the first hole, but never mind. I had one putt in this round on each of the first seven greens, varying from twelve yards to four feet, and in my 74 I took only 27 putts. In the second round I had a 73 and 28 putts, and I am naturally overjoyed to find that after a long lay-off through the summer I can come back to my croquet putting to find it foolproof against the jitters.
>
> I evolved a "sideways stance" as opposed to a "between the legs stance," which is the popular one in the Croquet Club. This stance, I find, gives me more freedom for the long approach putt— which all croquet putters for some reason that I have not yet discovered—find difficult.
>
> As I see it, the points in favour of croquet putting are:
>
> (1) It is foolproof against the jitters.
> (2) That the commonest faults in putting, (a) head up, (b) taking the club back outside the line, (c) moving the body, (d) no follow through, scarcely arise.
>
> This is a considerable statement, but I think anyone who tries croquet style putting will find it to be pretty well true.

I was surprised to find that great authority Mr. Bernard Darwin agree with me that croquet style had much to commend it. He went so far as to say that fifty years ago he felt sure that it was the best way of getting the ball into the hole.

Putting is always supposed to be related to billiards and good billiard-players often make good putters. It is of interest to me that this method of putting allows the player to have his eyes over the ball and the line of play just as those of the billiard-player.

One of the major threats to the ratings of televised golf is the interminable time spent by golfers on thinking about their shots. It is common for up to a full minute to elapse between the time a golfer's turn to play arrives and the moment he actually strikes the ball. While the camera lingers on the still life of a player in frowning concentration, the army of armchair watchers deserts by the thousands by switching channels.

Actually, this is the period when the *real* game is played. If expert commentators could read the minds of the players, and deliver blow-by-blow commentaries on the their examination and rejection of conflicting possibilities, the viewers would get a fascinating insight into the very heart of golf. What the golfer is doing during these *longuers,* of course, is forming a clear mental picture of exactly what he proposes to do, and why, and how. At least, that is what he *should* be doing, and the correct time to make the stroke is when the mental picture of the shot to be played has been clearly visualized, never before and never later. In practice players often need to do a little pacing up and down to compose themselves for the coming ordeal, but that is all part of defining the objective. First impressions are often most reliable, but there are occasions when the player does not form an immediate picture of the shot to be played, and spectators should extend their charity toward golfers who seem to have lapsed into a trance.

There is less justification for falling into a deep reverie after the ball has been addressed. Once you have settled on your chosen course of action, it should be a case of one or two practice swings if you like, just to remind the hands of the execution of the planned shot, then away you go. Waggles serve the same purpose of easing any tension in the hands and arms and of helping to formulate the approach line of clubhead to ball. But generally speaking, the longer you stand frozen over the shot, the less chance you give yourself to execute it successfully. There are exceptions in the case of outstanding individuals, such as Jack Nicklaus, but the same holds true of putts. The program should be to formulate a clear view of line and speed, then, having locked onto the target by setting the putter-head behind the ball, to play the stroke without further ado.

It really comes down to mental discipline, and for that reason the example of the South African champion Bobby Locke is worth studying. Locke was probably at his peak the finest putter who ever played professional golf. His technique may not be for you, but his routine remains a model for us all. Locke's calculations started as he walked toward the green, noting the general lie and the broad slope of the land. His survey of the putt looked leisurely, as he walked with the measured gait of a bishop advancing down the aisle, but his analytical mind was busily noting every factor that could influence the roll of the ball. As soon as he "saw" his line, he stood to the ball, made two practice strokes, then shuffled his feet an inch forward, and this time contacted the ball with his distinctive stroke. That routine never varied, from sixty-footer to tap-in, and though it seemed that he was playing slowly, his completion of the job so quickly once he reached the striking phase meant that he actually spent less time on his putts than many of the players who prowled briskly around the green and then lingered over the stroke.

It is a matter of personal preference whether you take one practice stroke or two, or use a deliberate forward press in the manner of Lee Trevino, or some other triggering device, but an established routine with a prompt stroke once you have made up your mind is well worth cultivating. And the same goes for every shot on the course. Also, you will be doing yourself and everyone else a favor if you begin your calculations while others are putting. Slow play is the bane of modern golf, and nothing wastes more time than the habit of waiting until it is your turn before starting to think about your shot.

Billy Casper is a fine example of golf's two phases. Once he completes the planning phase he goes into the execution phase with a routine as consistent and efficient as Locke's. Indeed, if Casper is disturbed during the execution phase he has to start all over again, replacing the club in the bag and, if necessary, having the caddie replace the head-cover. Then, when all is quiet, he reactivates his unvarying routine from the very beginning. That is discipline and proof indeed that it eliminates all doubts and uncertainties.

A word of warning may be in order to conclude this chapter. Putting is amenable to all manner of idiosyncracies because it is such an intensely personal activity. Famous players win themselves enviable reputations as fine putters and immediately they are recruited into the proliferating golf-instruction industry, retailing their secrets. The literature of putting instruction contains all manner of weird and wonderful ideas, many of which may well work for the authors: contact downhill putts off the toe of the blade to produce a soft stroke; adjust the stance for cross-hill putts; deliberately half-top short putts to impart overspin; hood the blade and aim for the right-hand side of the cup, thereby hooking the ball into the hole; and so on. Just because these ideas work for some individuals it does not follow that they should be incorporated into *your* game. They are complications, and the simplest way of putting is always the best way. Indeed, the examples quoted above are certain guarantees of confusion and indecision. Ignore them. Put your faith in a sure contact on the sweet spot and the doctrine that every putt is straight.

MY LOVE-HATE AFFAIR WITH THREE THOUSAND PUTTERS

I believe Palmer . . . was, and still is, the greatest natural putter of them all. He has everything it takes to get that ball from anywhere into the hole. Most of all he has the guts to get it up there and give it a chance.

—*Tommy Bolt*

When I produced my instructional book, *My Game and Yours,* I naturally included a chapter on putting. My friends gave me a hard time over that chapter. They complained that I advised my readers to grip the club any way that felt right, to stand to the ball in any manner that was easy and comfortable, and then simply to hit the ball. That is not instruction, they said, that's anarchy. Well, I stick by my story. There are no rules for putting except for the basic truth: if it works, it is right. If I see a young kid who belts the ball a mile but who has a fundamental fault in his swing, I urge him to make the necessary adjustment because it will pay off in the long term. But if I see a youngster who slots putts from all over the green while standing on one leg I might suffer a few pangs of envy but I certainly would not advise him to change his style. Come to think of it, standing on one leg to putt might not be such a bad idea; at least it would make you keep your head still.

After a fifty-year love-hate affair with putting, I am more convinced than ever that the only instructor who has the slightest chance of teaching you to putt is yourself. Putting is neither easy nor difficult: it is an instinctive function, like walking or talking, and the learning process is exactly the same. Try this experiment. Stand in front of a mirror and follow these instructions. Slightly open your mouth while curling your tongue upward. Do not allow the tip of your tongue to touch the roof of your mouth or the whole effect will be ruined. Simultaneously vibrate your vocal chords with a gentle exhalation, producing a tone in A-flat. Maintain that tone as you press the tongue against the hard palate and withdraw the tongue sharply with forward and downward flexion. Rest the tip of the tongue under the upper incisor teeth, raising the note a semi-tone. Pause for about a semi-quaver and press the lips together while keeping the teeth separated. Increase the pressure of exhalation as you abruptly release the air seal formed by your lips, reverting to A-flat. With the tip of the tongue resting against the back of the lower teeth,

force the lips firmly together momentarily, increasing the breath pressure as you drop the note of a semi-tone, and pull the chin sharply downward. Practice these moves individually until you are proficient with each stage. Then perform them in sequence at an even tempo, allowing 220 milliseconds between movements 2 and 3. Work at it for a few months and you might get the hang of it. Alternatively, you could just listen once to somebody performing that sequence properly, and then do it for yourself with a perfect enunciation of the words: "Arnold Palmer."

This second method was how I learned to putt. I watched my father putt, and I went out and did the same thing. The learning process was refined by experience. A six-year-old boy does not consciously remind himself to give the ball extra force for an uphill putt. The first time he has such a putt he leaves it short and his subconscious mind takes note of the fact. The next time he automatically hits the ball more firmly. Maybe it goes well beyond the hole. The subconscious mind makes another note. As the boy continues to putt, a constant stream of information is fed into his mind, where it accumulates into a sophisticated program that guides his actions. Adults marvel and exclaim that the kid has a gift. It is nothing of the kind, of course. It is simply an expression of the natural learning process, no more remarkable than the automatic response that prompts him to scratch an itchy nose.

I can't tell you how I learned to putt except to say that I absorbed the skill in the same way that I learned to walk and to talk, and not too long afterward, at that. At the age of three, too young to be allowed to run free without supervision, I used to trail around with my father as he worked on the Latrobe golf course. To the club he was the superintendent and pro, but to me he was a marauding Indian brave, or a pirate, or a bandito—any subject deemed suitable as a target for the pistols holstered on my hips. My standard equipment as a toddler were those guns and three cut-down golf clubs, including a putter with a brass blade.

There are only so many times that you can shoot your father in one morning, and on many occasions he did not present a suitable target in any case. This was long before the days of selective weedkillers, so the invading daisies and clover had to be removed by hand. String was stretched to section the green and make sure that no square inch was missed as my father and his men advanced laboriously on their hands and knees, jabbing with a fork so that the offending weed could be lifted intact from the turf without leaving pieces of root to grow again. So, while the adults went about their painstaking work, they offered no scope as fit subjects to populate the fantasy world of a three-year-old. No self-respecting cowboy shoots a man when he is on his hands and knees. Since I had to stay with them, I let my guns grow cool and devoted my attention to putting.

The one formal golf lesson my father gave me was to form my hands on the club in a conventional Vardon overlapping grip and announce in a tone that brooked no discussion: "This is how you hold the club." No child could ever receive a more valuable gift for golf than that basic grip, from which all golfing blessings flow, and naturally I held the putter the same way. Variations came later. For the moment, putting was just another game, and the learning process was completely subconscious. Obviously, I did not look for breaks or grain or think about the speed, although equally obviously I learned about them by the trusted process of trial and error. If I had to pick one factor that was responsible for my success as a golfer, I would unhesitatingly nominate an exceptional eye. By this I do not simply mean 20-20 vision, but a good eye in the sense that artists use the expression and, more important, a countryman's eye with its perception for the lie of the land and, more particularly, the fall of a green. That facility doubtless began to form in those early days during the weeding sessions, and it has strongly flavored my views about the game of golf.

Of course, golfers will always pace the course and consult their yardage charts, but I feel that golf is a better game played by eye. I like to *see* a seven-iron shot rather than measure it, and by the same token I do not think of clubs in precise mathematical terms. Playing by eye and judgment encourages a golfer to increase his repertory of shots, to manipulate the ball, which will make him, in my opinion, a more complete player. Often I take my seven-iron, for instance, for a shot that the yardage chart mechanics would insist was a natural six-iron distance, just as I contrive shots with a seven-iron that are standard eight-iron or nine-iron distances.

These days people would look askance at a tournament professional who copied Walter Hagen's habit of pulling his selected iron out of the bag as he replaced his driver. Such a cavalier approach would be considered highly unprofessional, although not by me. Hagen knew that his choice was near enough to what he was going to need, and he had the skill to play that near-enough club near enough to the hole. One of my ambitions is to promote a tournament in which the players will be limited to seven clubs. Then they will have to use their natural gifts rather than their pocket calculators, and they will have to improvise some real golf shots, the way the game ought to be played.

By the time I was seven my golf was proficient enough for me to play with the Latrobe caddies, who had to be over fourteen by law and many of whom were pretty handy players. This progression introduced me to the element of competition, which is the heart and soul of the game. Of course, I was outgunned by the boys twice my age, but that may have been a blessing in disguise in the education of a golfer. I formed the firm belief that if I could get the ball onto the green, even *near* the green, I had a chance because I could compete against anybody once the time came to get down to putting.

Nobody putts well every day. For some reason that has never been explained to my satisfaction the touch comes and goes, but by the time I started in high school just before I was fourteen and achieved my goal of playing number one on the school golf team in my first year, I had a firm notion of putting standards. A round of thirty-one putts was bad, a real bundle, and twenty-seven to twenty-eight was normal. My idea of a good putting round then hardly bears thinking about from the distance of forty years. Such is the innocence of youth. If I could recapture that precocious confidence on the greens I could still be contending for championships today. In those days I intended to hole every putt I addressed—and I mean *every* putt. My faith was not rewarded every time, of course, but the ball was either in the hole or right by it, and my belief that the next one would drop was never shaken.

Hope, the dreaded hope that replaces belief, was still in the future, and I was full of putting confidence when I won my first professional tournament, the Canadian Open, in 1955. At that time I was using a putter with a traditional blade, like Bobby Jones's "Calamity Jane," except that mine had a steel shaft. I had a phenomenal run with that putter, but never again was I to win a tournament that I could regard as predominantly a putting victory. After the last round in Canada I was checking my clubs before packing my bag and discovered to my horror that the magic wand had been stolen, never to be seen again.

One of the books I read as a boy was by Jones, every golfer's hero at that time, and how lucky we are that this fabulous player had such ability to express his ideas so clearly in print. Jones was the supreme exponent and advocate of putting to die the ball into the hole on the last gasp. That doctrine held no attractions for me. My temperament rejected it because by nature I had to give the ball a good run at the hole, and in those days return putts of four, five, and even six feet held no terrors for me. Intellectually, I also rejected the Jones approach because I had become thoroughly convinced by then of the advantage of having a firmly struck putt hold its line as it neared the hole. But I could not fail to be impressed by Jones's insistence on a pure and precise contact between club and ball. He stressed the need for keeping the body still during the stroke, and that I accepted without reservation. That conviction, reinforced by my experience, became and remains the bedrock upon which my action is based. It is easy enough to keep the body still on the practice green, quite another matter under the pressure of having "This for the Open." My stance evolved from my conviction that, although the head may move to follow the putt, the body mass must remain balanced and unmoving throughout the stroke. Hence the crouching, knock-kneed posture with the toes turned slightly inward. It may not be for everyone, but it works for me, and this part of my putting has never given me cause for further experiment. That, and the commitment to a bold run at the hole, have remained constants in my putting life and immune from tinkering.

What I wanted was a style that would enable me to get the putter back under the fiercest nervous pressure without any body movement. As for speed, I have always believed that getting the ball up to the hole with enough momentum to carry it two or three feet past was absolutely central to the whole game. Thus I worked very hard on schooling my feel for speed. If these are inviolates of my putting philosophy, I must plead guilty to much tinkering in other respects. In self-defense I will simply state that there is a world of difference between the swashbuckling putting ambitions of amateur golf and the agonizing necessity to hole putts in the professional game. Scientists may insist that a ten-foot putt is a ten-foot putt, regardless of where and when, and that the task of holing it is always identical. Don't you believe it! A ten-foot putt can be so easy as to be a mere formality, and that exact same putt can also be almost impossible, virtually beyond the power of mortal man.

Those do-or-die putts have two effects on the golfer: they ruthlessly expose any fraility in his technique, and they drain the confidence—drop by drop perhaps—but inexorably they erode the faith that is the greater part of putting. So eventually you tinker.

In my case, the tinkering was largely confined to the tools of my trade. Countless newspaper and magazine stories have commented, often in bemused tones, that the first thing Arnold Palmer does when he receives a new set of clubs from the factory is to put them in a vise and knock them out of shape. The armchair psychologists suggest that this is my way of imposing my will on the hapless implements, showing them who is boss right from the start. There might even be something in such theories, for all I know or care, but I do not tinker with clubs just for the hell of it.

Anyone of my generation who has been brought up at the clubmaker's bench acquires a feeling for golf clubs. It is not so long ago that all clubs were made by hand, and the master craftsmen of the trade did not use swing-weight and balancing instruments. They worked by feel and could detect minute variations in the limber of the shaft or the weight distribution in the head. I was raised in this tradition, which has survived the introduction of mass production and steel shafts, and I rely on my hands to tell me if a club is or is not perfectly tuned to my needs. With no club does this apply more strongly than the putter.

Over the span of my career I have accumulated about three thousand putters, many of them sent to me by well-wishers, and quite a few original designs incorporating some features the inventor thought would be helpful to me. It is true that I have used many different putters, and this might appear to contradict the advice to find a putter that suits you and stick to it. In fact, I have remained true to my first love in my fashion, as the song says, because I have sought to turn every putter into the original Tommy Armour flanged-blade model that served me so well in those carefree days when putting was a pleasure rather than a penance.

All my working putters have been replicas of Old Faithful, so far as I have been able to make them so, in feel and balance. The quest for the perfect putter has produced some odd results because tinkering is not an exact science. After I have filed away too enthusiastically to reduce weight, it has often been necessary to restore metal by welding. Then the weld has to be ground to shape and filed again. On one particular putter I repeated this process so often that eventually the head was almost entirely constructed of welds, with just a token nucleus left of the original steel.

It should not be thought that tournament golfers are immune from the human frailties that sustain the amateur's fantasy notions of finding the secret to golf. I have been equally guilty of searching for the putter that would work miracles, even though I know as well as anyone that the quest is absurd. There just are no miracles in golf. Even so, I continue to tinker and to keep an eye open for the putter that will rejuvenate my stroke. After all my exhaustive experiments with putters of different shapes and sizes and grip thicknesses, I have succeeded only in reinforcing my youthful instincts about the putter for me. Because I do not approve of making putters too complicated, it is basic: a simple blade with a flange to concentrate the weight low in the head and with a thin grip to allow maximum feel in the fingers. This may not be the putter for you, but in my case the wheel has gone full circle and I am back where I started, although for serious competition I have never deviated far from that concept.

The practice green is the place for experiment, except for those maddening occasions when you fall out with your putter and cannot do anything with it. It is surprising how often a change of putter will restore the winning touch, and, once that happens, it is often safe to go back to the regular putter. After all, a golfer invests an enormous amount of experience in schooling his hands to the weight and balance of his putter, and that investment should not be lightly discarded. One thing is certain: that new putter which gave you back your touch will not continue to produce consistent results. The rapport between a golfer and his putter may be a delicate relationship, but the feel of a long-used putter is programmed into your nervous system, and that is a valuable asset.

For this reason, I have never been one for selecting a special putter to accommodate abnormal conditions on the greens, such as choosing a lighter model for exceptionally fast greens. Better the devil you know, to do such delicate work: all the adjustments should be in making your judgment of how hard to hit the putt.

On the subject of fast greens, there is a school of thought in golf which holds that it is impossible to make greens too fast. Indeed, it seems almost like a competition at times between certain clubs as to which of them can capture the world record for the slickest greens: "These will give the pros something to think about!"

Well, there is some validity in the idea that fast greens are more difficult because they require more skill, but that notion cannot be infinitely extended. There comes a point of diminishing returns, when the importance of skill is replaced by sheer luck. That point is reached when the golfer is powerless to exert control over the ball, when a ball once set in motion goes on and on, often gathering speed as it rolls past the hole and clear off the green. We cannot put a precise Stimpmeter reading on that point and say that greens should never exceed a specific speed. The playability of a green must always be a combination of surface speed and the degree of contouring. A flat green can be extremely fast but entirely fair to the player, and Oakmont comes to mind as an example. But when the greens have severe slopes, such as those of the Augusta National, that same speed would be silly. The upper limit should be just before the skilled player loses the ability to influence the progress of the putt both for direction and distance. Unless those who prepare championship courses adhere to that unwritten rule, the game becomes ridiculous.

As for the written rules, they could do with some adjustment in my opinion. For instance, I find it inconsistent that the penalty for hitting a ball out of bounds is stroke and distance. It is true that I am never allowed to forget the twelve I took in the 1961 Los Angeles Open when I hit four shots out of bounds. Had the old distance-only rule been in effect, I probably would have made five at worst, but my opinion about the stroke-and-distance penalty is not special pleading. Nothing can change what is past. It is just that I think it is illogical that the penalty for hitting into a water hazard is stroke only, but when you fire one over the fence you suffer the double jeopardy of stroke *and* distance.

On the green I think it should be permissible to touch the line of the putt and press down anything, including spike marks, by using the natural weight of the putter. Under the present rules we are penalized for the uncouth behavior of golfers who scuff up the greens with their spikes, in some cases deliberately. I know that some people would surreptitiously exert downward pressure with the putter, but it is impossible to legislate against golf cheats. I would be prepared to give the cheats the benefit of the doubt in repairing spike marks, provided that the rest of us could legitimately press them down only with the weight of the putter. After all, what is the fundamental difference between a spike mark and a pitch mark? Both are caused as a result of normal play, and to me it doesn't make sense to allow repair of one and not the other.

It would make no difference to me personally to eliminate the penalty for striking the flagstick with a putt because I prefer to have the flag removed anyway. I would approve such a reform of the rules simply because it would remove one of the causes of slow play and also because it would save some of the wear around the hole. I cannot think that it would make any difference to putting. On balance, I would say that I have seen more putts from off the green stay out of the hole because of rebounding off the flagstick than I have seen putts that would have jumped over the hole hit the flagstick and drop. I seriously question whether anyone would deliberately charge a putt at an unattended flagstick and rely on the ball hitting the flagstick to halt its rushing progress. After all, that would involve exchanging a four-and-a-quarter-inch target for one half an inch wide, and that makes no sense at all.

It is no secret that there came a time in my career when, instead of believing that every putt was going to drop into the hole, I found myself just hoping some of them would do so. There was a Greek general who warned his troops against the dangers of hope. It was, he argued, the prelude to defeat because to hope was to admit the possibility of failure. As long as they believed in their invincibility, recognizing no other possible outcome but victory, they would always prevail. But to hope was akin to preparing a document of surrender for contingency purposes. That general would have made a great golfer, and I recognize in his philosophy my own attitude as a young man. I did not win every time I played, of course, but I believed I was going to, right up to the moment when such an outcome became mathematically impossible. There is no point in playing competitive golf, or any other sport, unless you are confident of victory. It is an insult to your fellow competitors or opponents not to try your hardest on every shot, and you do not play to the limit of your ability by just swinging the club and hoping for the best.

But, as I have said, the time came when hope entered into my thinking because my confidence had declined to the point that hope was the only emotion left to me. At that period I did give some thought to the arguments Gene Sarazen has been proclaiming for as long as I can remember. When the United States Golf Association made the 1.68-inch diameter ball compulsory, it did not enlarge the hole in proportion, retaining the 4.25-inch hole that had been used for the old 1.62-inch ball. Sarazen's campaign even included the promotion of a tournament for which holes of 8-inch diameter were used. Even so, Bill Melhorn managed to three-putt five greens.

And it is not just to preserve the ball-hole ratio that Sarazen wants a larger target on the greens. His case is that the small hole puts the accurate strikers at a disadvantage because, say, the man who hits a three-iron shot to twenty feet will need two putts and score the same as the inferior striker who misses the green, chips close to the hole, and takes one putt.

All that is true, and I do have a certain sympathy with Sarazen's claim that a slightly larger hole would encourage and reward more accurate approach play. But, on balance, I am not disposed to support his plea for a larger hole, even though it would be to my advantage. When I was putting well, before hope blunted my putting edge, I sank my share of those twenty-footers and so enjoyed the rewards of having found the green with the three-iron. In other words, for a good putter the hole is big enough. If it seems too small for me today it is because my putting is less deadly. So the ace putters beat me and, in all honesty, that is the way it should be. I have enjoyed the warmth of a hot putter, and it would be churlish to deny the same benefit to others.

We can take care of Sarazen's point about wild hitters chipping close to the hole by giving them a tougher shot from the fringe, and that is a simple matter of course preparation. I am all in favor of making the punishment fit the crime, while at the same time giving the golfer a chance to save his par with an exceptional recovery shot. Sarazen is really saying that it is wrong for a golfer who misses the green to get his par with a run-of-the-mill chip and putt. Very well, let's make him play an outstanding chip if he is to make par. Golfers have different strengths and weaknesses, and they should gain the rewards for their specialist's skills.

For the same reasons, I can't go along with those who complain that putting has grown in importance to such a degree that the balance of the game has tilted disproportionately in favor of the putting specialists. It is argued that in tournament golf the leading players all take much the same number of strokes through the green, and so the tournament comes down to a putting contest. In the first place, I dispute the selective statistics produced to support this claim. I have better ways of spending my time than fooling about analyzing golf scores, but I am quite sure that equally compelling statistics could be produced to "prove" that the leading players all take roughly the same number of putts and so tournaments really come down to long-game contests, or driving competitions, or iron-play tourneys.

The reason I am so dogmatic on this point, without benefit of mathematical evidence, is that I have only to reflect on my own experience for examples of tournaments in which different aspects of golf were paramount. Nobody realized at the time, nor will anyone ever know, how well I hit the ball in certain championships when my putting was off and thus my impact on those events was unremarkable. On the other hand, I have won on occasions when I was having trouble with some part of my long game but the putter more than atoned for those sins of striking. For instance, putting was an exceptionally important factor when I won the 1960 Masters, as it was in the reverse sense in the 1962 U.S. Open when I lost in a playoff with Jack Nicklaus. For the ninety holes of that championship I three-putted thirteen times and he three-putted only once. But there have been plenty of times when my putting was just average, neither extravagantly good or bad, when my success had to be attributed to solid play from tee to green, and I think particularly of the British Open of 1961 at Royal Birkdale, where the gale-force wind blew with a ferocity I had never experienced previously on a golf course. In any case, even if we accept those spurious figures and admit that the leading players take about the same number of strokes from tee to green, the tournament *ought* to be decided by putting. Putting is a very important part of golf and, other things being equal, it should be the decisive factor.

By nature I am conservative and thus reluctant to embrace change, and certainly not change for the sake of change. The game of golf has endured for several centuries in its basic form, and the torment of that four-and-one-quarter-inch hole is an integral part of it. It might be amusing once in a while to play to a hole five inches in diameter, or even six inches, but to me it would not be golf.

Gene Sarazen is not the only great player to have advocated some relief from the burden of putting. Ben Hogan once advocated that the golfer should be required just to get his ball onto the green, whereupon he would add two strokes to his score and march on to the next tee. Really! Of course, it is sad to see golfers reduced to quivering impotence by their inability to cope with the problem of putting into a four-and-one-quarter-inch hole and, next to old age, I dare say that putting miseries are the principal cause for giving up the game. Putting may be a prime cause of heart attacks, divorce, and insanity, and yet I cannot bring myself to countenance a change. It is because putting is so difficult, so demanding on human resources, and so critical to the result that it is vital to the game of golf.

My traditionalist attitude is not the only reason for rejecting any ideas about enlarging the hole. There is another compelling consideration. If you begin to entertain thoughts about the hole being too small, you are destroying your ability to putt. More than any other part of golf putting is a function of the mind, and it is to the mind that we must direct our attention if mastery of putting is to be achieved. As we have already discussed, the human brain is perfectly capable of reading the line of a putt, of working out the pace, of aiming the putter, and of executing the stroke, *provided the golfer lets his mind get on with the job without interference.* Thinking that the hole is too small is interference. Being critical of the condition of the green is interference. Believing a putt to be difficult is interference. Fear of a return putt is interference. Trepidation over leaving a putt short is interference. Dissatisfaction with your putter is interference. Reflecting that you will be dead if you miss this putt is interference. Wishing you could putt like Ben Crenshaw is interference. Believing that putting is too important is interference. Since it is a common condition for golfers to entertain all of those negative and destructive thoughts during the course of setting up for a putt, it is not surprising that so many putts are missed. What is surprising is that any putts are holed at all, especially when you consider that many a successful putt is the result of the happy circumstance of one error compensating for another.

The emergence of the specialist sports psychologist is a relatively new development and of undoubted value in some cases. But, of course, golfers have understood and self-administered effective psychological techniques ever since the game began. The earliest instruction books stressed the value of a correct attitude, and the best players knew instinctively what frame of mind produced the best results without having to read a book. In saying this I realize all too well that there is a vast difference between knowing that confidence is the golfer's staunchest ally and actually enjoying that confidence. Emotions cannot be conjured up to order, hence the joke about the suicidally depressed caller who was ordered by the telephone answering machine: "All lines to the Samaritans are engaged. You'll just have to pull yourself together and ring back in twenty minutes."

All that the golfer can do is to think rationally about the game and recognize that things are not good or bad, easy or difficult, but simply the way they are. Thus the four-and-one-quarter-inch hole is not too small or too big; it is just the golf hole. Accept it as such without attaching any emotional trimmings. In the same way, notice that the green is wet and leave it at that. Wet is neither good nor bad, just wet. And do not make a mental note to hit the putt

harder to accommodate the wetness; your subconscious mind is capable of making the necessary adjustments simply from the information that the green is wet. Dwelling unduly on the implications of a wet putting surface only serves to confuse your reflex responses.

Ideally, the golfer should keep his emotions in neutral, neither rejoicing over a successful putt nor despairing over a missed one. Of course, that is a policy of perfection which is beyond human achievement, but the nearer the golfer can get to it the better. The optimal mood for golf is a mixture of confidence in your ability and relish for the coming encounter. Once again, mood is not something you can pull on like a clean shirt. We have all stood by the first tee and read the telltale signs on a golfer who we know for certain is going to be in mental torment for eighteen holes and who consequently will have a horrendous score.

Just by thinking sensibly about golf you can help to achieve a positive mood. Count your blessings. Think how fortunate you are to be able to play golf at all. Anticipate the pleasures that await you. The purpose of golf is to generate pleasure, and it is worth reflecting that the odd setback on the course is necessary to enhance the satisfaction of the successes. The golfer who never missed a fairway or a green—or a putt—would quickly give up the game as being too boring. I have no time for those golfers for whom the game is a penance, forever complaining about the course and their play. In the case of professionals, it is no excuse for such people to say that golf is their job and they play it only for the money. It is a sin, in my firm conviction, to play golf and not enjoy it. If mood cannot be summoned to order, it can be encouraged if the golfer shrugs off the failures and allows the successes to inspire him.

Anyone can imagine the lift I received when my opening drive for the last round of the 1960 U.S. Open reached the green of the 346-yard first hole at Cherry Hills. On that occasion I had little cause to relish the coming round because I was seven strokes behind the leader and nobody gave me a chance to make up such a deficit on Mike Souchak. In fact, I was in a buoyant mood before that round because the prospect of golf has always created a tingle of anticipation in me. Perhaps it is my good fortune that I have always enjoyed the feeling of setting out on a challenging voyage of discovery every time I played, even in quiet social games with friends, but that opening drive at Cherry Hills certainly intensified my normal eagerness for the encounter. The pinprick of light at the end of the tunnel is never entirely extinguished for people of truly competitive nature, no matter how bleak the situation, and now I detected a positive gleam. The rest is history.

Another success that I must ascribe to a positive attitude was the 1962 British Open at Troon, now Royal Troon. The course that year was parched, and the ball bounced alarmingly, sometimes in eccentric directions. I did not like those conditions one little bit, and it would have been all to easy to succumb to a fatalistic mood, telling myself that golf on such fairways is little more than a lottery. There is no doubt that many of the players fell into that very mood of negative fatalism. I determined to approach the championship positively, reflecting that my game was particularly suited to such conditions. Missing a fairway would be no big deal because I was young and strong and the desiccated rough held no terrors for me. It was an exercise in kidology, but that is the very message I am trying to convey. I convinced myself not just that I could win but that I was *going* to win. That mood of confidence paid off, most notably with one of the best putting championships of my career, and I had the additional satisfaction of relegating to second place the Australian Kel Nagle, who had pipped me by a stroke in the Centenary Open at St. Andrews two years previously.

I also set a then record for the championship winning total, but that may have been a mixed blessing. Naturally that record was a source of considerable satisfac-
tion, and inevitably it came to mind when I took a substantial lead in the 1966 U.S. Open at the Olympic Club in San Francisco, leading by seven strokes with nine holes to play and with the U.S. Open record total in my sights. I would have been inhuman not to have reflected on the prospect of setting new standards for the world's two greatest championships, a double of which any golfer could be justly proud. That incentive certainly did not dominate my thoughts, but the passing notion was enough to deflect me from my real purpose, which was winning. In that regard, thinking about record scores is interference! Instead of applying myself to each shot, one at a time, I had allowed my mind to race ahead in anticipation of triumph, always a fatal mistake in golf.

There is no greater test of a golfer's spirit than to stop the rot when a comfortable lead begins to dissolve, as panic and despair strike the vitals. Once more, it takes little imagination to share my feelings over those closing holes, or to understand how Billy Casper drew inspiration from my failings. Anxiety affected my putting in particular, so we can add another candidate to the list: anxiety is interference. Downs are as much a part of golf as ups, and the proper response to both is the same: learn from them but do not brood on them.

The euphoria of yesterday's triumph is a dangerous passenger to take onto the course today, and so is the dismay of yesterday's disaster. The golf ball does not appreciate that you are a hotshot player, nor does the golf course. It is a clean sheet every time you play, and you have to impress them with your talent all over again. Nobody ever hit a ball with his reputation. As with most golf subjects, Bobby Jones had the correct attitude about mistakes. He did not welcome them, of course, but when they came along, as they must for every golfer, he analyzed them on the grounds that you learn nothing from a good shot but that a mistake gives you an opportunity to learn something that will improve your game. Did I learn anything useful from San

Francisco? Well, just put me in the Open with a seven-stroke lead and nine holes to play again, and I promise that I will not let that opportunity slip a second time.

The vogue these days for sports psychology is an entirely natural development since golf is played mainly in the mind, although I must say that I don't applaud the increasing tendency of tournament professionals to acquire a traveling retinue of caddie-chaffeur, golf coach, and personal psychologist. The high priest of the movement is Timothy Gallwey, and his teachings about the inner game have been rightly acclaimed. I absolutely endorse his ideas, but then I did so long before he wrote them, just as every successful golfer before me employed the same valuable psychological techniques.

I am quite sure that Old Tom Morris was a fine exemplar of the inner game, and, of course, Walter Hagen was a supreme master of mind over golf. As for Gary Player, he was always a better striker—and putter—than he was given credit for, or, indeed, than he himself claimed to be. But as a sports psychologist he is the world champion in the heavyweight division. Of course, we did not think of it as psychology, nor did we consciously analyze the way we thought about playing the game. But we reached the same end result instinctively.

It may be said that if I had been taught about the workings of the subconscious mind as a boy, that understanding might have provided a few shortcuts to success. I doubt it. Success came quickly enough. The young need no urging to follow the dictates of their subconscious selves, and formal teaching on this subject might well create confusion and actually hinder their progress. Experience is the surest tutor. Many times I have been in difficult situations and found myself wondering how to play a shot and reflecting that when I was a kid I would go ahead and hit the ball without thinking about it. That's it! There is the secret. The trick is to define the objective. Think about the exact shot you want to hit, and then go right ahead and swing at the ball without thinking about how.

In the same way, I have often reflected ruefully after missing a putt that, in the old days, I would have holed out without trying. That's another secret. The way to hole a putt is not to try. Just *do* it. Everyone knows about the dangers of trying too hard. All that happens when you try too hard is that you get tense and nervous and you miss. But trying is like hoping, in that it contains the damaging seed of doubt about the success of the enterprise. The basis of golf is to be absolutely sure in your mind about what you intend to do and then to rely on your instincts to guide your actions.

Of course, as a youngster I did not ponder deeply on the relationship between the conscious and the subconscious, or explore the nature of ego and superego. I did not even think about why I played golf in a certain way. I just *did* it, and only now do I understand that by not thinking about it I was using sophisticated and highly scientific psychological techniques!

One of the best-known tricks of self-kidology, advocated from the times of the earliest teachers, is the key thought for the day. For putting, it might be to keep the back of the left hand moving along the target line. These key thoughts often work wonders for one round but then lose their potency if you persevere with them, and for obvious reasons. If you get a fixation about the back of the left hand, pretty soon you will transfer the responsibility for the stroke from the master hand to the left hand, and your putting will go to pot. I have used many key thoughts, and my policy was always to choose some detail of the stroke which I knew to be an important element in a good swing. So, one day I might concentrate on a light grip, switching to a steady head over the ball for the next round.

A useful key thought for putting on many occasions was to focus my attention on one individual letter of the maker's name on the ball. In the course of time, however, I made what seemed to be a most curious discovery: the key thought for the day need not be a vital component of the stroke. The system worked just as well if I thought about something that contributed nothing to the stroke, such as concentrating fiercely on my toenails. I pursued such experiments by selecting a subject that had nothing at all to do with golf. Mysteriously, it still worked. I had an excellent putting round, I remember, by visualizing the line and strength of my intended putt, taking my address, and then giving my full attention to the task of making an anagram from the names of my playing companions. A name like Weiskopf can keep the attention truly occupied.

It takes an expert such as Timothy Gallwey to explain this phenomenon, although it becomes obvious enough after you hear the answer. Provided it has absorbed all the relevant data about distance, slope, grain, and texture, the subconscious mind can work out where to hit the ball and how hard and it can guide the stroke as surely as it transports a fork-load of steak to your mouth without stabbing you in the chin. But if you start giving conscious instructions and warnings about not being short and making sure to take plenty of borrow, the subconscious mind becomes confused. And so we are back to interference again. Since the mind can handle only one thought at a time, those key thoughts have the effect of blocking all interference until the ball is safely on its way. Instinct then has a chance to do its job properly.

So now we have a working doctrine for putting: don't hope, don't try, and don't second-guess your vision of line and speed. Stick with your first impression and, if you must think, then think about something that cannot possibly influence the putt.

If by chance the ball does not drop, do not turn away in disgust as you realize it is going to miss. Observe how the ball behaves because that may have an important bearing on your next putt. If the putt breaks much more sharply than you anticipated, you need to be forewarned for the return putt. Do not reproach yourself for having

misread or mishit the putt, and resist any temptation to replay the putt. All that does is to delay play, and golf has become interminably slow as it is. Keep calm and tell yourself that you hit a perfect putt and some blemish in the green must have deflected it. Your subconscious mind will learn the necessary lesson without any outside help, and the next putt really will be perfect.

All this talk of perfect putts prompts me to reflect that I am advocating a doctrine of perfection for what we all know to be an imperfect world. It is not the easiest thing in the world to abandon all conscious responsibility for your golf and let your instincts have their head. Perhaps that is the way we walk and talk and read a book, but golf is too important.

Golf is the measure of a person. It engages pride and self-esteem, and it establishes status within the tribe, or so the player feels. Actually, nobody thinks any the worse of a golfer because he is less than a scratch player, but we are terribly self-conscious about not making fools of ourselves on the golf course, even if such foolishness is a figment of our imagination. That is why golfers hope, and try too hard, and think hard about every slightest element of the action they are about to perform, and, in short, do everything that, together, guarantees they will make fools of themselves. And it has to be said, with due deference to the proponents of instinctive golf—among whom I number myself—that there are some great players who prefer conscious control over instinct. In particular, I think of Dr. Cary Middlecoff and Jack Nicklaus, whose approach to every shot reminds me of an airline captain doing an exhaustive cockpit check.

What the majority of professionals seek to do is to practice until they reach the point that a swing or a putting stroke becomes simply second nature, that is, it is so deeply imprinted on the subconscious that it will repeat automatically forever and a day. Unfortunately, it does not work out quite like that, although good golfers do have streaks when they do not think about striking and thus can concentrate entirely on the more important subjects of where to hit the ball and why. But even when he is on a roll, Jack seems to be paying conscious attention to every detail of his game, and this is particularly true of his putting. Nobody needs me to tell him what a formidable performer on the greens Jack is, with a well-earned reputation for holing them when the heat is turned up the highest. How can he succeed when he deliberately interferes with the proven method for success, while others who let the subconscious mind have its head so frequently fail? Well, there is another factor in the equation: nerves.

Everything about golf—attitude, technique, imagination, intellect, composure, instinct—can be destroyed in the devouring flames of fear. Bobby Jones insisted that it was inappropriate to talk of fear in golf because the golfer is never in physical danger. But there are many forms of fear, and golf offers a wide selection: fear of losing, fear of making a spectacle of oneself, fear of a high score, fear of losing face, and, above all, fear of being seen to be afraid. The symptoms of these fears are just the same as those suffered by a soldier pinned down by enemy fire: dry throat, perspiration, trembling limbs, and loss of capacity to think rationally. So, when nerves afflict the golfer—and it happens to all of us—all those lovely theories about the conscious and subconscious mind fly out the window. They become casualties of nervous tension because the nervous golfer can neither think straight nor hold the club still.

The first thing to understand about nerves is that they are no cause for shame. Fear is a natural response, a valuable warning system for self-preservation, and the effect of fear is to sound a call to action stations to the body. Fear closes down all its unnecessary functions and optimizes those functions needed to fight or to flee. One important effect for the golfer is an increase in the hormone adrenalin, which creates a sudden increase in physical capacity. That is why parents are capable of unprecedented feats of strength, such as lifting an automobile off a stricken child, and why golfers find themselves hitting the ball much farther than usual when they get into clutch situations.

Experienced players learn to recognize the symptoms of nervous tension and to take appropriate countermeasures, such as selecting one or more less clubs than usual, gripping lightly, and being sure that they complete the backswing at their familiar tempo. Nobody is immune from nerves, and certain players welcome them. I think particularly of Gary Player, Jack Nicklaus, and Lee Trevino in this context. They thrive on the stimulus of nervous excitement and frequently play better for it. Of course, familiarity with the situation helps, and a golfer's nervous threshold rises with experience. Once you have experienced the nervous pressure of your first tournament, your first time in contention, your first win, your first chance at a major championship, your first victory in a major, your nerves progressively subside. But for those golfers who need the inspiration of a nervous tingle, that progression reaches a point of diminishing returns. Nicklaus no longer gets a charge from the general run of weekly tournaments, and so he can rarely produce his best form in them. He plays a limited schedule of Tour events to support the sponsors, but he is reluctant to put sub-Nicklaus golf on public display. His main purpose is to sharpen his game for the major championships that still retain their thrill for him. I understand his attitude even though it is very different from my own.

One way to control the damaging effect of nerves is to understand how they operate, and why, and also to adopt the slightly arrogant attitude that if you are feeling nervous, the others must be equally affected, and more so (of course they are more affected because they're not such steely characters as you). It does no harm at all for a golfer to believe himself to be superior to the others, and, indeed, it may well be essential for a champion to hold that view. The important thing is to keep such a notion well buried in the secret recesses of your private being and never to exhibit it publicly. Golf has an unerring capacity for knocking arrogance out of a player, and so it helps when you do run into some devastating humiliation if you have at least preserved a facade of modesty and humility. That way you will be hurt inside, but at least the blood will not show. Also, you will be a far more pleasant character to your companions and friends.

Although the physical changes that occur in the body in response to pressure can be beneficial to the full swing if properly exploited, the same is by no means true of putting. There is no advantage in acquiring the ability to hit a putt two hundred yards, and it must be admitted that putting becomes virtually impossible when the club in your hands feels, in the graphic phrase of the late Henry Longhurst, like a live snake. But, it *does* help to confront your fear and rationalize it. "OK, so I am nervous. That means, among other things, that I will have a tendency for the muscles to tighten, and in any case the nerve endings near the body surface will become dormant and I will lose my feel." Simply recognizing the condition often helps it to subside, at least to some extent.

There is also one very good trick to counter the tendency for the muscles to tighten, and that is to forestall the natural effect and deliberately to tighten the muscles at the start of your routine. Grip the putter as hard as you can. Tighten every muscle in the body. Then relax this tension and go into your usual routine of addressing the ball, taking your practice stroke, then hitting the ball.

But the most valuable specific against the effect of nerves is the accumulated experience of all those hours on the practice green. The scientists call it psychophysiological autogenesis, and we golfers call it muscle memory. Either way, it means that if you repeat an action often enough, it will become second nature and you will even-

tually repeat it automatically. That is why we pros try so hard to groove our swings and our putting strokes by constant repetition. Nobody ever completely succeeds in turning golf into an entirely spontaneous and natural exercise, but the ones who look most natural, like Sam Snead, are the ones who have put in the most work on the practice tees and greens, hitting and stroking hundreds and hundreds of balls a day. They are often described as "naturals," but I would not advise anyone to say so to their faces. They have all, without exception, invested years of their lives, usually on a daily basis, in the hard labor of acquiring that natural appearance. Nothing pays off like practice in this game, and that goes for putting just as much as it does for trying to belt drives over the perimeter fence.

At tournaments it is common to see a player who has finished his round out on the practice green hitting putt after putt to one hole. There may be sixty or seventy balls clustered around the hole, and many times I have heard spectators comment that it seems futile to continue putting to a hole that is truly blocked by golf balls. Besides, it would surely be more sensible to vary the practice and play to a different target with each putt, thereby acquiring a feel for speed and line. The spectator has missed the point because in this case the player is working solely on his stroke. Holing out is irrelevant to this exercise because he is concentrating on grooving his stroke and making a good contact between the sweet spot of the putter face and the ball, while keeping the putter head low to the turf on the backswing and follow-through. He is working to commit his action to his subconscious mind, so that it can do the business without any outside help.

That is just one form of putting practice. Feel and touch require other exercises, so now there is virtue in varying the putts, best done by scattering practice balls in a circle or crescent and putting them to a common target so that each putt will be subtly different. The best method is to stick rigidly to your on-course routine with each ball, visualizing the line and then going into your inflexible sequence of address, practice putt, and putt. Some people find it valuable to look at the hole for the practice putt because this gives the subconscious mind a final reminder about the distance. Others swear by the technique of schooling their awareness of line and distance by closing the eyes to putt on the practice green, and a few brave souls have actually employed this method on the course. Another method is to line up the putter square to the target, then to fix the eyes on the target while making the putt. I am prepared to accept that such experiments on the practice green may help a player acquire the precious feeling that the putter is an extension of his body, to the point that he is virtually rolling the ball up to the hole with his hand. Obviously, in my never-ending quest for a sure-fire putting system, I have tried all these ideas at some time, and just because I have settled for different exercises does not mean that they may not be beneficial to you. In any case, a golfer learns something every time he hits the ball, and he learns the most valuable lessons from the swings and putts that do not work.

Ever since I achieved some prominence in golf my mailbox has been swollen by letters from well-meaning correspondents anxious to confide the secret of golf. The rate of these suggestions has never dropped to less than one or two a week, and during periods of my well-publicized slumps the flow has surged to flood proportions. A random sampling of recent offerings has included the advice to relax the tension in my shoulders at address, to overlap two fingers of the right hand as a guarantee against missing the hole on the left, to line up putts using the right eye only, to stick fishing-line sinkers at either end of the blade, and to wrap a bandage around my left forearm to prevent rotation of the ulna and radius bones.

Many of these helpful hints are accompanied by vivid accounts of miraculous performances by the inventors, although I must say I entertained certain reservations about the account of one sixty-two-year-old correspondent who described how he had just driven all the par-fours on his course, thanks to having discovered the secret of golf, namely playing every shot on one leg. Another self-confessed champion, this time in putting, said that the trick lay in immobilizing every muscle in the body except for the upper left arm. Push the putter back on a generous backswing, he urged, then let gravity do the rest.

One writer offered as credentials that he had read four books that had convinced him that the human mind was capable of exerting control over inanimate objects, including golf balls. There is a certain merit in another proposal, to pick out an aiming mark on the turf about six inches in front of the ball, then, having squared the blade, to focus on that mark, not looking at the ball again until lifting it from the hole. If only it were that simple!

On the mind-over-matter theme, a correspondent wrote that he had cracked the problem of putting. All you had to do was to look at the hole and imagine it growing bigger and bigger. Once it reached the size of a washtub, it was simplicity itself to knock the ball into it. That is a lovely theory but, in practice, the hole has a perverse habit of looking smaller and smaller until it seems to heal over, leaving not so much as a scar on the turf to show where it had been located.

But I think my all-time favorite was the forthright critic who addressed me tersely: "It seems to me that you need to work not only on your game but also on your head." Amen to that. Nobody can deny that, with putting, success and failure are dependent on the human head rather than the putter head.

THE AGONY
AND
THE ECSTASY

Relaxation is absolutely vital. I believe this facility for keeping oneself relaxed at all times adds a great deal to the pleasure of living.

—Bobby Locke

You better believe it

"There's a ball in here somewhere, guv'nor, down among the fishes." Caddie's version of the cliff dive at Acapulco during the 1961 British Open.

Photographers have been giving me the business for the best part of half a century. Apart from odd incidents, such as the time when an over-enthusiastic cameraman crawled into a bunker with me during a British Open Championship to get an atmospheric shot full of flying sand, I have managed to coexist with them pretty well. And they do perform one special service. People always assume that golfers are like fishermen in that they exaggerate their triumphs and disasters. Well, the camera cannot lie. For instance, if I tell you that the storms were so rough during the British Open at Royal Birkdale in 1961 that the golf course was transformed into a lake you might be tempted to think I was laying it on a bit thick. But here is the proof, and I remember it well. And in the pages that follow you do not have to take my word for it that golf can be a pain as much as a pleasure. You can see for yourselves, thanks to the photographers. So share some memories, both good and bad, from the scrapbook of an itinerant golfer.

Waiting for the wind of

We have all seen young children screw up their faces in perplexity over a difficult word when reading a book. When it comes to reading greens it appears that I am still a child. Somewhere on that treacherous page of trim green turf there is a line, an invisible path that leads to glory. But where, oh where, is that elusive line? We can only hope that concentration will result in comprehension. I am not sure that there is any particular lesson to be learned by golfers from these seven pictures of concentration, but brain surgeons might pick up a hint: evidence that mental confusion activates the facial muscles.

British Open, 1982.

World Match-play Championship, 1983.

The Masters, 1982.

PGA Championship, 1984.

The Masters, 1983.

The Masters, 1985.

And the old bullfrog waiting to pounce. But in which direction? British Open, 1982.

Spot the difference

The difference? Well, here I am missing a putt on the front nine during the 1966 U.S. Open at the Olympic Club, San Francisco, but still stretching my lead to seven strokes during the final round.

And here I am missing a putt on the back nine on the way to blowing that entire lead and the championship with it. The pictures may appear much the same, but in this second shot the internal bleeding was worse.

Spot the similarity

Contrary to all appearances I am not auditioning for the lead tenor's role in Rigoletto. Your second guess, that I am possibly about to throw up, would be nearer the mark as another putt slips past the hole.

This one too has a hint of the theater about it, a suggestion of James Cagney stopping a .45 slug in the back. That is how it felt at the time, but the wound healed when they dressed it with a green jacket, at the 1962 Masters.

Sometimes you lose

Sometimes a miss doubles you up like a hairpin, as here during the British Open of 1981 at Royal St. George's.

And sometimes it gets you right between the shoulder blades, the way it did at Medinah in the U.S. Open of 1975.

Sometimes you win

Happier days, at the inaugural World Match-play Championship at Wentworth, England, on the way to victory in the final.

This short putt, with quite a swing on it, safely found its way below ground for my second Masters title in 1960. ▼

Some moments to remember. Tango time on the way to a fourth Masters in 1964.

When life is sweet, brother

Going great guns in the 1975 Masters ...

and a punch to celebrate another birdie in the second round.

MASTERS OF THE BLACK ART

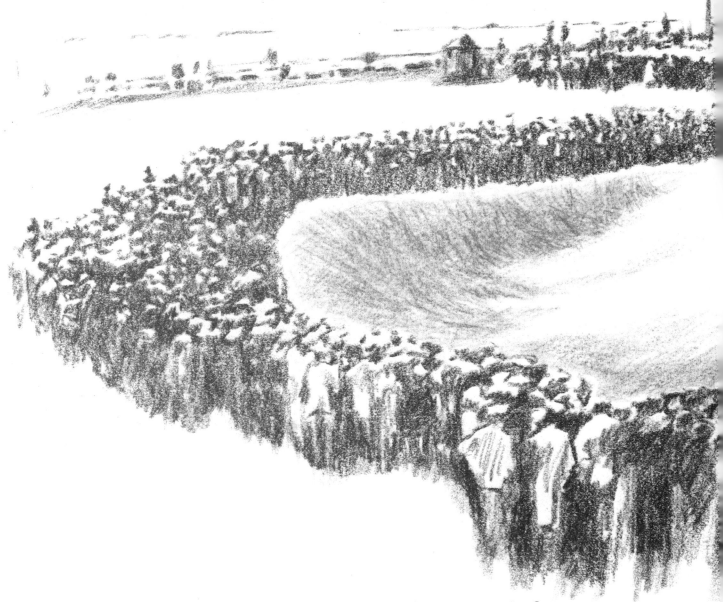

The man who can putt is a match for anyone.

—*Willie Park, Jr.*

Books and instructional articles in golf magazines are a source of fascination for golfers who seek to improve their games, and there is no doubt that the written, and illustrated, lesson can be enlightening. That, after all, is the only justification for inflicting yet another instructional book on the golfing public.

Yet there is a danger, as we have constantly stressed, in dogmatic statements about putting. What is truth for one person may well be fallacy for another. There is no consensus in putting. It is possible to take a dozen instructional books by famous players and to abstract a set of golden rules for putting that are advanced with all the authority of the ten commandments. Alas for the poor reader, the commandments vary from book to book.

Thus we are exhorted to stand with feet together (Max Faulkner), four inches apart (Bobby Locke), at shoulder width (Billy Casper), or widespread (Ruth Jessen). The head should be positioned behind the ball (Jack Nicklaus), or above the ball (nearly everyone else). The weight should be slightly on the left foot (Gary Player), or evenly distributed (Bobby Locke). The ball should be played opposite the left toe (Bruce Devlin), opposite the left heel (Dai Rees), or in different positions according to the type of putt (Gary Player). The putt should be hit on the downswing (James Braid), on the upswing (Tony Lema), or at the bottom of the swing (Sam Snead).

What is the confused reader to make of all this? The answer, as we have stressed, is for him to undertake his own consumer research, to put every suggestion to a field test on the practice green, and to retain only those tips that prove successful in his own case. In the pages that follow a brief analysis is made of the styles of some of the foremost putters in the game. The intention is not to present a distillation of absolute truth about putting, but rather to set out a window display of classic fashions for the reader to assess and adapt to his own special taste and needs. These word-portraits are not intended to be comprehen-sive, for such a task would be repetitious and exceedingly dull, but to highlight distinctive features of each method in the hope that somewhere you may find the perfect accessory to complete your golfing ensemble.

BOBBY JONES

These days it is impossible to conceive of an amateur, and mainly a weekend golfer at that, winning a major championship, let alone thirteen of them, including the Grand Slam. There is, therefore, a tendency among young players to imagine that it must have been much easier to win championships in the days of Bobby Jones, that the courses must have been set up as benevolently as possible, and that the opposition must have been weak. In fact, in some ways golf was more difficult with hickory-shafted clubs, balls of uncertain quality, and courses that did not enjoy the benefits of automaic irrigation systems and modern greenkeeping aids. Yet Jones dominated championship golf more completely than any player before or since. He was probably the most complete golfer who ever lived—supreme thinker, supreme striker, supreme putter, and supreme sportsman—all of which is more remarkable because he suffered from nervous tension to a degree that rendered him incapable of keeping food in his stomach before an important round.

Jones wielded his famous putter, Calamity Jane, from a markedly upright stance, with his feet almost together and his left elbow pointing along the target line in a modified version of Leo Diegel's idiosyncratic spread-elbow style. He was the high priest of the smooth stroke school of putting, and when he retired from competitive golf, he wrote eloquently and prolifically about golf technique. What follows are extracts from his instructional articles, selected to illustrate different aspects of his putting philosophy.

ON GRIPPING LIGHTLY. "There is nothing more important to remember than a

Bobby Jones

light grip when one runs into a streak of bad putting. When the little ones begin to slip past the hole and the stroke feels a bit uncertain, there comes a great temptation to tighten the grip, shorten the backswing, and try to guide the ball into the hole; the fact that a similar procedure has failed innumerable times seldom prevents our trying it once more. The truth is that a putt can be successfully steered no more than any other golf shot. On the putting green, as elsewhere, the only hope of success lies in a smooth, accurate stroke that permits the clubhead to swing freely. When we become afraid to trust this swing, we can expect trouble."

ON JABBING. "A backswing that is too short goes inevitably with a grip that is too tight. No one ever stabs or jabs a putt when the club is held gently, and the arms and legs are relaxed; but always something goes wrong when he drops down on the club, crouches low over the ball, and hits it sharply, with the idea that he won't give the face of the club a chance to come off the proper alignment."

ON TENSION. "I liked to feel a tiny flick of the right hand as I struck the ball. I know of no better way of describing the mechanics than to say that the left hand controls the path of the stroke, and the alignment of the face, while the right hand supplies the touch—that nice adjustment of speed that rolls a long putt to the edge of the hole.

"To avoid freezing, I liked to keep my knees loose and mobile. It is not a matter of putting with body motion, but of keeping the legs and trunk responsive and ready to move if there should be the slightest suggestion that it may be necessary for them to do so. In other words, there should never be any attempt to putt with the wrists alone, or even with the wrists and arms. When making a very short putt, there may be no movement above the hands, but that is only because no such motion is necessary."

ON CONTROL. "The most helpful single thing I was ever able to do to my putting style concerns the left elbow. I found that by bending over enough to produce a decided crook in both arms, and by moving my left elbow away from my body until it pointed almost directly toward the hole, I was able to create a condition of relaxation and easy freedom I could get in no other way. Although I should, by that time, have learned how deceitful are the gods of golf, I could not resist the temptation to write that this came very close to being a panacea for all putting ailments.

"The reason for the beneficial effect is that this location of the left elbow places the left hand and wrist under perfect control. I liked to make good use of my left hand in putting, but I knew it caused me many unhappy days, because of its tendency to turn over or to pull the club in as I tried to swing it through—a kind of involuntary flinching that can be ruinous. With the elbow out and the left hand gripping the club so that its back is presented squarely to the hole, I found that the tendency to turn or flinch was almost entirely eliminated."

ON FOCUSING. "Once the club has moved away, it is the back of the ball, the thing that is to be struck, that holds the player's attention. The expert golfer senses through his hands the location and alignment of the face of the club throughout his entire swing. Naturally he is going to look at the thing he intends to hit, and at a point where he intends to strike it. He would be no more likely to look at the front of the ball than he would be to look at his thumb if he were hammering a nail."

ON PUTTING PRACTICE. "A whole lot of the art of putting depends on judgment, nerves, a sense of touch, and, as much as anything else, upon luck. By far the most important part is a sound stroke, by means of which the ball can be struck smoothly and accurately most of the time. Judgment of speed and slope count for very little without the stroke to back it up.

"For this reason, there is no finer practice for developing a reliable putting stroke than putting without a hole—just dropping a number of balls on a green or a carpet and stroking them back and forth. Relieved of the need for finding and holding the line, the entire attention can be given to the club and the manner of swinging it."

"Now begin swinging and continue with the motion that you are trying to cause the head of the putter to float through the ball. Banish any thought of tapping the ball, sharply or otherwise; in fact, try to forget there is a ball there. Your aim is to swing the head of the putter, and the more freely you can cause it to swing, the better will your job be done.

"Strive to make the club swing in a flat arc; that is, to keep it low going back and coming through. Try to swing through the ball, keeping the sole of the putter close to the ground, and direct the swing precisely along the line upon which you intend the ball to start. Above all, let the club swing freely without arriving at any abrupt stopping place."

ON SHORT PUTTS. "The short putt presents a problem, because if we allow for the roll of the green, the stroke must be so delicate and the blow so gentle. To strike a crisp, firm, and at the same time gentle blow requires the very ultimate degree of what we call touch, and firm hitting is the essence of good putting.

"On a keen green, putts of a yard can be terrifying, especially in medal or stroke competition. The player always has the choice of striking firmly for the back of the cup if he does not like the delicate curling attempt—but then he must think of the putt he might have coming back if he should miss the first.

"The mental attitude in which we approach a short putt has a lot to do with our success. When we walk up to a putt of ten or fifteen feet, we are usually intent upon holing it; we know we shan't feel badly if we miss, so our entire attention is devoted to the problem of getting the ball into the hole. But it is quite different when the putt is only a yard long. Then we know that we ought to hole it easily, and yet we cannot fail to recognize the possibility of a miss. Instead of being determined to put the ball into the hole, we become consumed with

the fear of failing to do so. Our determination, if we may call it such, is negative. We are trying not to miss the putt rather than to hole it. A casual tap with the back of the putter is enough to hole any short putt when no one cares whether it goes in or not, but once large issues are placed upon the results, two hands and a world of pains are required to steer the ball into the hole."

ON CONSISTENCY "I wonder how many putts that are holed follow exactly the path laid out for them in the player's mind. I should say that as many of those that go down deviate from that path as follow it. It appears to me that the good putter is simply the man who can keep coming close— who gets more times within one-foot radius—and that such a man holes more putts because, of the greater number that come close, a greater number more likely will go in.

"Working on this idea, it must appear that we should concern ourselves mainly with the more general contours of a slope rather than to try to account for every little hop or roll the ball is likely to take. This does not mean that we should be taking a haphazard shot at the hole, but only that we should determine a line upon which we want the ball to start and hit firmly upon that line. Worrying about rough spots in the green has no effect except to make the stroke indecisive, and I believe that bad putting is due more to the effect the green has upon the player than to that it has upon the action of the ball."

SAM SNEAD

The popular view of Sam Snead is of a man who was born with a gloriously natural and classical swing but who never quite had the putting touch to match. On both counts this judgment is wrong. Nature gave him a wonderful physique and temperament for golf, but the swing was the product of long and intensive labor. Likewise, although he had spells of increasingly serious problems on the greens, it is ludi-

Sam Snead

crous to imagine that anybody could win more than 150 tournaments, including the British Open, 3 Masters titles, and 3 PGA championships, without being an outstanding putter when the going was good.

At the age of thirty-four, when he had been a professional for twelve years and had won nearly forty official PGA tournaments, thanks in large measure to brilliant putting, Snead engaged in a series of sixteen challenge matches in South Africa against Bobby Locke. Snead managed to win two of the matches and squared two, but the venture was a huge success for Locke, who was thereby emboldened, with Snead's encouragement, to try his luck on the American Tour, which he pillaged so thoroughly that he was eventually declared persona non grata. The cause of Snead's failure in that series was the onset of the twitch, which was all the more apparent by contrast with Locke's mastery. Snead spent two years in the doldrums before a change of putter restored his touch and started the most prolific winning spree of his remarkable career. It did not last much more than two years, and then that putter broke. A new shaft did not help. The magic was gone, and Snead was painfully reminded of Tommy Armour's famous dictum: "Once you've had 'em, you've got 'em."

Golfers are slaves to fashion, no less than any other section of the community, and in his early years Snead was a hands-and-wrists putter, in the style of Bobby Jones and, later, Billy Casper. With clinical observation worthy of a medical researcher, Snead deduced that his malaise afflicted only the smaller muscles, so the first remedy he adopted was to grip the club tightly, thereby immobilizing the afflicted muscles, and to employ a stiff-wristed style of arm putting. Very sensibly, he persuaded himself that this was a more reliable method anyway, especially under pressure. Being an experienced professional with a marvelous eye, he made it work, at least long enough to make a massive addition to his formidable array of titles. Then, during the 1966 PGA Championship, the yips re-

turned. Snead jerked one putt and actually hit the ball twice on what was technically the same stroke.

With his experience of the pathology of the twitch, Snead immediately realized he must devise a method of putting that would not involve any of the affected muscles. On the next green he stood astride the line of his putt and played the ball with a croquet stroke. He adopted the croquet style as his routine putting method and soon was back in business as a tournament professional. Then the ruling bodies outlawed croquet putting and Snead had to think again. He recalled an "old-timer back in England" who would bet that he could out-putt anyone with his variation of croquet putting. That old-timer was almost certainly Leonard Crawley, the former Walker Cup player and golf correspondent of the *Daily Telegraph*.

The variation of style used to circumvent the ban on croquet putting was to address the ball outside the right foot instead of between the feet. Snead quickly picked up the method, and it did not take him long to appreciate the special virtues of what he called side-saddle putting, which the press quickly revised to sidewinder putting. For sufferers from the yips or twitch, the advantage is that the yipping or twitching muscles are passive during the stroke. There are no moving parts among the afflicted regions because the putter is moved to and fro along the line with a straight right arm, in much the same action as rolling a ball up to the hole from the hand. Snead further claims that when you face the hole, it is easier to see the line, to move the putter head along it, to contact the ball on the sweet spot, and to avoid the risk of quitting on the stroke because of the natural tendency to accelerate the clubhead through the ball.

The side-saddle style of putting will always be associated with Snead, just as the conventional golf grip is associated with Harry Vardon, although neither originated the method. But they popularized these valuable advances in golf technique, and spreading the word is as important as writing the word. In the case of Snead, side-saddle putting underwrote a distinguished extension of his career, bringing him victories as a senior with scores that increasingly beat his age. He wondered why he had ever started putting in the conventional style in the first place, which is quite a recommendation from a man who was a dominant figure in tournament golf for half a century.

BOBBY LOCKE

Bobby Locke started playing golf at the age of four with a cut-down jigger. Five years later, he was on the practice green of Germiston golf club in Johannesburg, still trying to putt with this less than suitable implement. A group of members watched the lad's efforts for some time from the veranda, and then one of them, a T. D. Lightbody, who had just bought a new putter, called out to Bobby: "Would you like to play with a real putter, son?" Bobby gratefully accepted the loan of Lightbody's old putter, which he had decided to throw away in any case. Bobby putted with it for about an hour, then came back to return the putter. Lightbody told him he could keep it.

Thus was formed the most famous partnership of player and putter in the history of golf. With that old hickory-shafted blade putter, Locke won four British Open championships and fifty-five tournaments around the world, including eight South African Open championships, two as an amateur, and eleven American PGA tournaments.

Locke had an acute golfing mind and an unflappable temperament, and he played every shot with a pronounced hook—draw is much too mild a word for the great curving shots he controlled with such uncanny precision. His real forte, however, was on the greens, using a stroke that was a miniature version of his full swing and as individual to him as his white cap and voluminous plus-fours. His contemporaries were unanimous in acclaiming him the world's finest putter, and his method is best described in his own words:

First of all, I grip the club in the left hand, and the grip is normal except that I position my thumb down the center of the shaft. The art of putting lies in the tips of the fingers. If you have a delicate touch, you are lucky. It helps a great deal. But remember you must not grip tightly. You must grip loosely and do everything possible to acquire a delicate touch.

The shaft of my putter is much longer than the standard men's length. I find that this gives me what I call "better head feel." I grip my putter at the very end of the shaft and I use the same grip for all putts. Never change the position of the hands up or down the shaft whether it is a long putt or a short putt, as it will cause inconsistency. With the right hand I use the overlapping grip as for all other clubs, but again the thumb is placed down the center of the shaft. Having the two thumbs in this position enables me to follow the clubhead through dead in line to the hole.

Most putts are missed not because they are mishit but because they have been started on the wrong line and at the wrong speed. I examine the line of the putt, concentrating particularly on a radius of about three feet around the hole. This is where the ball completes its run, and what happens here is going to make or mar the putt. During this quick inspection I remove any obstacles which might deflect the run of the ball, but, more important, I check the pace of the green, determine how closely the grass has been cut and whether the green is fast, slow or medium-paced. Also I check the lie of the turf around the hole to see whether the ball will be going slightly uphill or downhill or dead level as it approaches the hole. It is at this stage that I determine how hard I am going to hit the ball, always, of course, taking into consideration the length of the putt.

I work to the rule that if the green appears to be fast, I will aim my putt at an imaginary hole six to twelve inches short of the hole. If the green appears to be

slow, and particularly if during the last two or three feet to the hole the ground is up-hill, I hit it firmly for the back of the hole.

I now get behind the ball to examine the contour of the part of the green my ball will have to cross. Chiefly I am concerned with slopes and any hills and hollows. According to the slope, I make up my mind on the direction of the putt, whether it shall be dead straight or whether I should aim for the right or left side of the hole. Once I have made up my mind as to the line of the putt and how hard I am going to hit it, I never change my mind. It is fatal to let second or third thoughts intrude as you are putting. You must make up your mind before you begin to address the ball, and never alter it.

The weight is evenly distributed on both feet. I place the feet about four inches apart, with the right foot about three inches behind the left in relation to a straight line from the hole to my left toe. This is known as a closed stance, and I adopt this to prevent myself from cutting across the ball and imparting any side-spin. I position the ball directly opposite the left toe. This enables me to hit the ball slightly on the upswing, whereas if the ball were farther back towards the right foot, there might be a tendency to top or jab it. I begin the address with the ball opposite the toe of the putter but actually strike the ball with the center of the blade. I do this to avoid cutting the putt.

If one addresses the ball with the center of the putter blade, there is a tendency to swing outside the line on the backswing, resulting in a cut and the ball not running true. By addressing the ball near the toe of the putter blade it is easier to take the putter back "inside" the line of the putt, and in this way one is able to impart top-spin at impact. Never hit a putt with the heel of the club. That puts check on the ball and it will not run as far as you expect.

On the backswing I keep the putter very low to the ground, almost brushing the turf. I am careful to take the putter back to the "inside" and there is no wrist work at all. Throughout the swing, the putter blade stays square to the hole. I want to emphasize that the blade does stay square to the hole. There are people who say it is impossible to take a club back "inside" without opening the face. With a putter it is not impossible, and this is how I putt. I learned the method largely from Walter Hagen in 1937. The term he used for taking the club back and still keeping it square was that you "hooded" the face. The putter, left hand and left arm to the elbow, are in one piece. To make sure that the clubface does not open, the back of my left hand keeps pointing to the grass.

At impact I keep the left wrist firm in relation to the forearm; the position of the left hand in relation to my putter is exactly the same. This means that the putter blade is kept square to the hole. My head is kept well down until the ball has been struck. On the follow-through I concentrate on keeping the clubhead square to the hole and on keeping my head well down. It is only necessary to follow through as far as the club went in the backswing.

My method of swinging the putter is the same as the swing of a clock pendulum. It cannot be too much emphasized that the putting action must be slow and smooth, and above all the grip must be loose to maintain the most sensitive touch. My putting is based on the fact that there are three entrances into the hole, three chances providing the speed is right. There is the front door and there are two side doors. Obviously it is safest to use the front door, but, with my method, if the ball catches the side of the hole it will fall. By thinking of these three entrances, I always feel that I have three chances of sinking every putt.

JACK NICKLAUS

What are the images of modern golf? Gary Player punching the air? Lee Trevino briskly setting up for an iron shot with the ball in a position that would be beyond both the reach and the imagination of most players? Arnold Palmer's distinctive twiddle of the clubhead at the end of an-

Jack Nicklaus

other storming drive? The intensity of Severiano Ballesteros as he scents yet another victory?

For many people, the most evocative scene of the modern era would be of Jack Nicklaus going to work on the birdie putt he needs to win a championship. It is a classic study in concentration and meticulous preparation. Those who know him best claim that he has never hit a careless shot in his life, and that may well be the case. Before he plays any important tournament he studies the golf course more thoroughly than any other golfer. If players were required to take a written examination after every tournament, Nicklaus would get top marks every time; he could produce an accurate plan of every hole, complete with an inventory of grass species, shrubs, and trees, as well as a topographical survey of the site down to the subtlest slopes of the greens.

Much of the information he acquires in his preliminary reconnaissances is of no practical value during play, but these fact-finding missions are rather like packing for a long vacation. You can never be quite sure what you might need, and Nicklaus sets his mind at rest by taking everything that might conceivably be useful. For instance, not many golfers are aware that trees of the eucalyptus family are inordinately thirsty. You can be sure that Nicklaus knows—and perhaps once in his career has benefited from the knowledge—that a shot pitching near a blue gum tree will get more run than usual because it is landing on ground that has had more moisture drawn from it than the rest of the course.

Nicklaus leaves nothing to chance because such an approach to his profession would be anathema to his nature, and this facet of his character is never more apparent than when he putts. He is, most obviously, absolutely insulated from his surroundings. There may be twenty thousand people surrounding the green, but they do not exist. His fellow competitors evaporate from his consciousness. Even his caddie is banished, out of sight and out of mind. Nicklaus is alone within his cocoon of concentration, just him, the hole, and a corridor of green back to his ball. These are not just the most important things in the world for the moment; they are, in a very real sense, the *only* things in the world.

We all eat apples without giving much thought to it because there are millions and millions of apples and always will be. But imagine that some pestilence eliminated apples from the face of the earth and then, ten years later, you came across a lone survivor, one tree bearing a single ripe, red apple. You would look at it with a rare intensity, seeing it in a new light and appreciating the beauty and texture of the fruit for the first time because, in a sense, this is the first time you had actually looked closely at an apple. And the taste! How you would anticipate sinking your teeth into its flesh and how your palate would respond to the sweet acidity of its savor.

It is this heightened awareness which Nicklaus seeks to achieve as he observes a putt and ponders the effect of break and texture. You can detect the moment he determines the line by the abrupt way he takes his putter and moves into the execution phase of the task. As he settles over the ball he seems to be checking the position of every joint in his body, making tiny adjustments of the feet, arms, and hands. He himself denies this interpretation, surprisingly for a man who is so calculating and practical in other matters, insisting that his putting is largely inspirational.

Nicklaus crouches with his eyes directly above the line of the putt, but behind the ball with his head slightly cocked to the left, the reverse of his practice on full shots when he cocks his head to the right. The temptation is to say that he now freezes over the putt because he stands stock still for a very long time, sometimes in the past for up to a minute. But freezing implies paralysis, and Nicklaus is not immobilized. What is he thinking about during these periods of suspended animation? He does not know; he is not even aware of the passage of time. All he can tell you is that he waits until he feels *ready* to putt. When that moment eventually arrives, he takes the putter-head slowly back along the line and then reverses its direction at the same leisurely pace.

Nicklaus does not appear to make a conscious hit; the action is more of a sweep along the line on which his ball happens to be sitting. The other powerful impression he gives is that willpower takes the form of a physical force in his putting, with the ball being guided between the rails of twin laser beams from his unblinking gaze. That is a fanciful thought, if you like, but it is undoubtedly true that, contrary to the general rule, Nicklaus putts best when the nervous tension is highest, and the same goes for the rest of his game. Down the years, he has maintained a uniformly high standard of putting, and an analysis of those championships he has lost by a stroke or two reveals the cause to be excessive caution with the long game rather than deficiencies on the greens. But if you abstract from his career those pivotal pressure putts that made the difference between winning and losing, then Nicklaus's putting is phenomenal.

What lessons may be drawn from his putting that might be of value to the average golfer? Well, it is an individual method evolved for the purposes of an exceptional individual. It is based on self-control of a very high order, control of both mind and body, and it is probably true to say that only a Jack Nicklaus could master it. That does not preclude others finding equal success with his method, but they will, by definition, be very rare animals indeed.

GARY PLAYER

The world has a distressing and undiscriminating habit of accepting people according to their own valuation of themselves. Thus the world does not think of Gary Player as an exceptional putter be-

cause Player himself does not go around boasting that he is the greatest putter who ever lived. Player is justly proud of his prowess as a bunker player because he is a magician from the sand, but otherwise he is modest about his golf and thus is not particularly perturbed when the pundits complain that he often hits the ball when he is off-balance—indeed, to hear Player himself talk sometimes, you would think that he is a martyr to an uncontrolled hook on every shot.

There is one man, however, who has an extremely keen appreciation of every facet of Player's golf, including his putting, and that is his bank manager. Being a true professional, Player is content with that single endorsement of his method. In fact, Player is a fine example to all golfers because he exemplifies the paramount importance of attitude. He is the outstanding proof of mind over matter in golf, and the strongest element in his mind is an exceptional competitive spirit. None of us enjoys being beaten, but to Player winning is life itself. In his self-deprecating way, he says that he adopted his rap style of putting because the greens were so bad when he was a boy in South Africa that he could not develop the smooth stroke of the master putters for whom he has so much admiration. As with many of Player's public utterances, a certain amount of interpretation is necessary to discern his meaning.

Player is not above waging a degree of psychological warfare with his opponents, and it gives him a buzz of malicious pleasure to extoll the superior putting talents of his rivals and then go out and putt them off the golf course. He has done that many times, most dramatically in fighting back from seven down to beat Tony Lema in winning one of his five World Match-play Championships in 1965, and again in the 1978 Masters, when, eight strokes behind the leader at the start of the final round, he went through the field like an avenging angel to win for the third time.

As with all his numerous international victories, these triumphs were testimonials

Gary Player

to Player's indomitable will. Psychologists see him as a classic case history of the undersized weakling who determines to meet the giants on level terms and beat them. His fanaticism for physical fitness and insatiable appetite for the practice ground were the outward expressions of his combative nature, and these are the reasons he cites for his success. But ambition and relentless tenacity were the real driving forces, and he showed these attributes from his earliest days as a golfer, particularly on his first visit to Britain, when an experienced professional took one look at his swing and, with the kindest of intentions, advised him to return home and get himself a club job. The effect on Player was merely to harden his resolve to improve his technique.

In his practice putting sessions he liked to play against an opponent, with enough of a wager on the outcome to induce tournament tension. He putted for more than he could afford to lose, and in the early days that was precious little financially, but it was not the money so much as self-esteem that was the real prize. Player would go on and on, into the night if necessary, putting by the lights from the clubhouse window, until he was on top. His reward might be no more than a shilling, but he had earned the richest prize of all—the satisfaction of winning. He had surmounted another obstacle on his way to the top.

The method forged in these competitive fires was conventional enough, but Player put deep emphasis on what he considered to be the critical elements. The head must be positioned with the eyes directly above the ball. There must be no movement at all of the head and body during the stroke and, like George Low, he favored the weight on the left heel to stabilize his stance. The putter-head must be kept low to the turf on the backswing and follow-through to prevent any tendency to lift the head before contact. Player favors a slightly wristy action for long putts, but once he gets into reasonable holing range, he adopts a short rapping action.

Unusually, Player varies the ball position according to the type of putt. For straight ones he plays the ball from a position opposite his left toe, but if the putt is going to break left he positions the ball back in his stance, just inside the left heel, to ensure that his hands remain ahead of the ball and will therefore be less likely to pull the putt left. If the putt breaks to the right, he positions the ball outside his left toe because he feels that this prevents him from pushing the putt out to the right.

Most golfers disapprove of the practice of sizing up the line of a putt by observing it from behind the hole, on the grounds that it cannot do more than confirm the impression you have already formed from looking along the direction of the putt and that it might actually confuse your reading of the putt. Player likes to assess his putts from both directions and then, having settled on the line, to pick out a spot on the green about two feet in front of the ball as a point of aim.

Above all, he guards against the defeatist attitude of questioning the value of giving your whole heart and attention to putting when the greens are bad. If you think there is no point in giving a putt your best stroke, you certainly will not make a good stroke. From there on the rot goes through your entire game because, as you miss putts, your confidence evaporates, and then your entire game goes to pot. You have to believe.

BILLY CASPER

During his prime years Billy Casper had an ambivalent attitude toward the golfing public's view of him as an ace putter. He was flattered that this part of his game had received due recognition, but at the same time he resented the implication that all he could do was putt. After all, the finest putter could not win a tournament unless he had the shots to put him into position to get to work with the putter, and Casper's record

Billy Casper

spoke for itself. In winning the U.S. Open championships of 1959 and 1966, Casper played 162 holes of golf, and he had single putts on fifty-four greens, a notable testimonial both to his putting and to his approach play.

Casper's philosophy of putting was that it was essentially an exercise in feel, and all his efforts were concentrated on maximizing his sense of touch on the greens. His stance and address position varied from day to day according to how the mood took him because, in his mind, such things were largely irrelevant, within reasonable bounds. His concentration was focused on the relationship between his hands and the clubhead, and to this end he gripped the putter in the fingertips rather than the palms.

Casper was probably the most famous exponent of wrist putting, although this is something of a misnomer because on the longer putts he employed considerable arm movement. But when he was in the holing-out range, he restricted movement to a hinging of the wrists, with a short backswing and a curtailed follow-through. Over the short span of this movement the clubhead was kept low, almost brushing the turf, and, indeed, his stroke frequently ended with the clubhead resting on the ground.

It can be well appreciated that this style, being totally dependent on the small muscles of hand and wrist, requires the most precise control, and, if attempted by players of less phlegmatic temperament than Casper, could be highly vulnerable to nervous tension and thus definitely not a technique for the faint-hearted. Indeed, Casper himself had his off days like everyone else, but this had nothing to do with changes in nervous control. It is a well-established fact that sensitivity of touch varies from day to day, and nobody knows the reason, or all the reasons, for such discrepancies. Biorhythms? Metabolism? Mood? The answers may be there somewhere, but for the moment they are unexplained.

At all events, Casper's touch was good enough often enough to make him one of the outstanding putters of the postwar era and one of the very few who emphasized the dominant role of the left hand, both in pushing the club back and pulling it through again.

BOB CHARLES

It is a matter of public record that Bob Charles, the tall left-hander from New Zealand, was the outstanding putter of his day, just as it is a matter of observation that his style is one of classic simplicity.

From a markedly upright stance, Charles grips the club with his right hand (remember that he is a southpaw) in such a way that his arm and the putter become an entity, a solid limb that has no joints or moving parts except for a hinge at the shoulder. The motive power for this inflexible limb is his left hand. He swings that extended arm back, then pushes it through the ball, and, provided he holds that right shoulder-hinge steady, the method is foolproof. There is nothing to go wrong because the system is mechanically perfect.

Perhaps it is because the style is so sound that Charles dismisses the importance of technique. After all, he does not have to think about technique, any more than the doorman at the Ritz has to concern himself with such considerations as whether the hinges of the door have been properly aligned or whether the door will return flush to the door-post after he has opened it to admit a guest. Such things do not enter into his consciousness, and it is the same way with Charles when he is putting. Nevertheless, his advice on how to putt is no less valuable because he dismisses the physical activity as being of minor importance. Indeed, it may well be all the more valuable for that very reason. Charles says:

Technique is no more than five percent of putting. It is nearly all in the mind. The overwhelming factor in putting is to believe that the putt is going to be successful. I am not saying that it is necessarily

Bob Charles

Isao Aoki

easy to achieve that conviction. Nor does it always happen by any means that even when you do believe that the putt will drop that it does so. Nevertheless, your belief has to remain unshaken next time. One way to confirm your belief is to make sure that you have an absolutely precise intention of where you intend to hit the putt, of course. Believing is all. Once that confidence goes then you cannot putt. It is as simple as that.

ISAO AOKI

Like all boy caddies down the ages, Isao Aoki spent every spare moment of his time at the Abiko club chipping and putting with any club he could lay his hands on. He thus acquired a short game in the best possible way, by trial and error, at a time when his mind was not cluttered by theory and notions of correct style, and his only consideration was the results.

An American serviceman who was one of Aoki's regular clients gave his clubs to the youngster when his tour of duty was completed. Being a full-sized set, the clubs were much too long for the diminutive child, who had then not shot up to the height that was to earn him the nickname the "Tokyo Tower." Accordingly, Aoki had to wield these clubs in an excessively flat arc, or he would have been digging into the turf with every stroke. Here, then, was the genesis of the most distinctive style in modern golf, particularly noticeable in the putting stroke.

Aoki addresses the ball with his hands held low and the ball well in front of him, with the result that the toe of his blade is cocked high in the air. His stroke is almost a chop as he takes the club back with a de-liberate lifting action that emphasizes hand action, and there is a distinct pause as he stands motionless with the club poised. Then he returns the clubhead to the ball on a downward path, thereby breaking yet another rule, that the putter-head should be kept low to the turf both back and through the ball. Indeed, there is very little

in Aoki's putting that conforms to normally accepted principles of good putting, but he does do one thing that is emphasized as the highest ideal of putting: he gets the ball into the hole.

Aoki's rating in the official PGA Tour sta-tistics for 1983 as the best player of bunker shots and the second best putter on the tour is eloquent testimony to his sensitive touch. He is often described as being a natural golfer—or of being exceptionally gifted, which is a variation on the same theme—and there is no doubt that he did inherit his share of the natural faculties needed for golf. But, above all, Aoki is a graphic example of a player who learned golf during his formative years and without the benefit—or interference—of conven-tional instruction. His method may be un-orthodox but it passes the ultimate test with honors: it works.

TOM WATSON

Tom Watson is quiet, unassuming, and modest, and when he is pressed to talk about his ambitions he speaks of striving for perfection in golf technique. People tend to take him at face value, and since we all feel more comfortable once we have mentally attached a label to a person and assigned him to the appropriate pigeon-hole, Watson gets rubber-stamped—"Man-ner and appearance of superannuated choirboy, classic swing, unflappable tem-perament"—and he is filed away alongside Gene Littler and Don January.

The time is overdue for a reassessment and a new label for Watson. In the Central Casting computer of the public mind Wat-son should be reclassified as "Yorkshire terrier type, fearlessly aggressive." The man who presents the image of a sporting angel is in reality a guy who dashes in headlong where angels fear to tread. He belongs in the pigeonhole occupied by Gary Player, Arnold Palmer, and Severiano Ballesteros, and this well-hidden streak in his personality is the key to his golf, including his putting.

Tom Watson

Watson's style is the modern orthodox arm-and-shoulders pendulum, with the wrists firm, and his philosophy is that a four-foot return putt is infinitely preferable to a one-inch tap-in from in front of the hole. Where he differs from most pendulum putters is that instead of controlling the movement of the club with the master right hand, he supplies the guidance with the left hand. Indeed, he practices short putts holding the putter with the left hand only, to intensify the feeling of guiding the clubhead through the ball with that hand. The function of the right hand is simply to impart the impetus of the hit at impact. He belongs to the school of thought that advocates a short backswing to ensure the clubhead accelerates through the ball.

SEVERIANO BALLESTEROS

The Jesuits say: "Give us the child until he is seven," implying that by then he will be secure in his faith for life. There is a distinguished body of players whose experience suggests that the same is true of golf. Harry Vardon, Bobby Locke, Dai Rees, Arnold Palmer, and Severiano Ballesteros were all hooked for life by the age of seven, and their skills were acquired in the best way—they learned golf rather than being taught it.

If the golfing Jesuit wanted to set a boy on the road to the heights of championship glory, he would have to specify a particular type of child, a lad with a victory fixation, an absolute obsession about coming out top dog in any enterprise he chose to undertake. Given that precondition, it would not be necessary to provide anything very extensive by way of equipment and opportunity.

That is the way it was with Ballesteros. He inherited a double helping of consuming ambition, and he acquired the cast-off head of an old three-iron. That is all it took to create a champion. He pushed a stick into the hosel of that clubhead and hit stones with it around the family farm at Pedrena on the northern coast of Spain, aping his older brothers who were working their way up to professional qualifications as caddies at the golf club in Santander. This golfing environment did not much help the young Severiano, and more than enough obstacles were put in his way to test his resolve, even when he acquired a proper three-iron and real golf balls to hit on the beach. In turn, he too became a caddie, and, like all caddies the world over, he chipped and putted in desperate matches against the other boys under the pressure of playing for pesetas he did not possess.

Ballesteros worked out his own salvation for each golfing problem as it arose, and with the pragmatism of youth he had only one test of technique: Does it work? Inevitably, that test produced the same results which generations of great players had evolved over the centuries, with one notable exception. On breaking putts, Ballesteros deliberately hooks and slices the ball, hooding the clubhead at impact for right-to-left putts and opening the blade for left-to-right putts. He scorns scientific proof that sidespin cannot influence the run of a putt once the ball has started rolling. "I do not believe the scientists," he says, adding a personal truth that totally discounts the discredited laws of nature: "Besides, hooking and cutting the ball improves my feel." There's confidence for you.

Ballesteros is certainly an exceptional putter, and the key to his success, he believes, is keeping a perfect pendulum action, with the clubhead moving backward and forward the same distance, at the same speed, and at the same height over the turf.

GEORGE LOW

In the years following World War II, George Low was a successful tournament professional, and, though he could hold his own with the best over seventy-two holes, he realized that he could beat them like a

Severiano Ballesteros

George Low

drum at his specialized skill of putting. So he retired and became a putting professional, making a comfortable living by giving lessons to anyone who cared to seek his advice.

Since one important element in putting is the tension of competition, Low's lessons almost invariably took the form of a challenge match. He was never beaten over the long haul of what he considered to be a fair contest, his definition of a fair contest being as long as it took for his challenger to raise his wallet in the traditional gesture of surrender. Low's reputation as the world's best putter was nearly unanimous, and Low himself was never slow to advance his claim to that title because it was good for business. Like the mythological gunslingers of the Old West, golfers who fancied their chances on the greens sought to topple Low from his perch, and he invariably cut them down to size, sometimes contemptuously completing the job by discarding his putter and kicking the ball into the hole. He became so famous for this trick that a major footwear company put him under contract to promote its golf shoes. He became a familiar figure on the practice putting greens at tournament sites, and, apart from his big-money matches, was always ready to give advice to professionals who seriously sought his help.

Although Low insisted that putting was an individual talent, and that his way might not necessarily be suitable in every respect for other golfers, some of his main precepts coincided precisely with the method advocated by Bobby Locke.

On the subject of feel, which he considered to be the keystone of putting, Low used the analogy of picking a particular coin from your pocket. How do you perform that operation? You grasp each coin between the crook of the index finger and thumb, identifying it with the pad of the thumb because that is the most sensitive area of the hand. So he gripped his putter with both thumbs not stretched down the shaft but slightly retracted, or short, on top

of the shaft, employing a standard interlocking grip. His putter grip had a flat top to maximize his thumb feel, and he always held the putter at the top of the grip, since moving the hands up and down the grip changed the balance of the club and his aim was to eliminate as many variables as possible. As for grip pressure, he likened putting to playing a violin, holding lightly for the softer strokes required on fast greens and delicate downhill putts but increasing the pressure for fortissimo putts on slow greens and also for the decisive stroke on short putts to direct the ball firmly into the cup.

At the address, Low withdrew his left foot slightly, giving him an open stance for improved comfort and a better line of vision from ball to hole. To block any body movement and eliminate any tendency to sway, he settled his weight, which in later days was considerable, on the left heel but without any tendency to tilt.

One very important point Low made about the stance was always to make sure to line up parallel to the starting direction of his intended putt. So many putts failed, he observed, because players lined up parallel to the line to the hole, even though they proposed to putt wide of the hole to take account of the break.

With the ball opposite his left instep and the arms close to his body, Low concentrated on making the same stroke every time. He likened the putt to a swinging gate, which comes inside on the backswing and then, after a fractional pause to assist the tempo, returns square to the ball, or gatepost. To help him take the clubhead back on the inside, Low addressed the ball off the heel of his putter. He found that this helped him make impact with the sweet spot at the center of the blade, ensuring solid contact.

Although Low was quintessentially a stroke putter, he emphasized the need for a positive hit at the ball. He used the analogy of driving a tack into the back of the ball for a solid contact, even on the shortest putts.

MARK G. HARRIS

Who is Mark G. Harris? How many championships did he win? What is he doing in this pantheon of prodigious putters?

Do not scoff, for, with Mark G. Harris, we are in the presence of true greatness. Throughout this book we have focused mainly on tournament professionals because they are household gods, their methods are universally available for inspection and analysis, and their results are a matter of public record. Mark Harris was a private citizen whose skills were revealed to the world only once, back in the thirties.

Now, let us dispose at once of the inevitable objection that no one can be regarded as a good putter unless he has proved himself in the ultimate test of putting, under the unique pressures of championship golf. Granted that a putting method cannot be endorsed until it has demonstrably stood up to the rigors of nervous tension, but championship golf is not the only method of inducing tension. After all, golf is only a game. A man would be under much greater strain if an executioner stood by to shoot him if he missed a twelve-footer. And the test to which Mark Harris was subjected was certainly comparable to, if not sterner than, having "This for the Open." Mark Harris performed under the petrifying gaze of that Cyclopean monster, the film camera of Paramount Pictures. And, as testified by eyewitnesses, there was no hanky-panky with retakes.

Harris was a portly Chicago businessman, who in 1923, at the age of sixty-two, received from his doctor a stern ultimatum: "You are heading for an early grave with that heart flutter and your general state of poor health unless you quit work immediately, retire to a benevolent climate, and take it easy. The very minute you start any funny business, don't hold me responsible."

Harris did as he was bid and took himself off to California, spending an inordinate amount of his time in restful tranquility on a patio overlooking a miniature golf course by the Hotel Ambassador in Los Angeles. After four years one tends to run out of conversational subjects with the same circle of friends, and Harris increasingly turned his attention to the golfers who passed within his view. He announced to his incredulous friends that he proposed to take up the game. Their unanimous verdict was that he was mad. He made a spirited reply in self-defense: "If a man has a live spirit, a perseverance that never falters, and the know-how to do things right, he can do almost anything, even at sixty-six." Harris then returned to Chicago, inquired who was the best professional in the city, and sought out the man recommended, Bob MacDonald, lately of Dornoch, Scotland, and now the chief instructor at an indoor golf school. MacDonald was impressed by the determination of this unlikely pupil. After receiving his necessarily rudimentary grounding in golf, Harris returned to California and went to work on his game. The reputation of his phenomenal short game began to spread and, in due course, reached Paramount, which decided to make a short feature film of his prowess on and around the green.

Harris displayed his full repertory of touch strokes for the camera at the Rancho Park golf club. Chipping from the fringe at thirty-five feet with his mashie, he holed one shot and put the other two within a foot of the hole. From forty-five feet he chipped in once and put the other two balls within fourteen inches. He was given three balls to demonstrate his putting, and he holed all three from eight feet, repeating that success rate from fourteen feet. Then, to demonstrate that the four-and-one-quarter-inch hole was really too generous a target, he stuck a tee into the turf and played three putts from a range of seven feet, hitting the peg with each ball and at a speed that left no doubt that it would have dropped into a regulation cup.

Did he just have one of those days, showing off the for sake of the camera? According to contemporary witnesses, including the noted amateur champion George Von Elm (who asked him for les-

Mark G. Harris

sons), Harris played to this standard all the time. Bob MacDonald said of his pupil's skill: "The putting stroke of Mr. Mark G. Harris is the most phenomenal and nearest to perfect I have ever seen." And George Von Elm added his personal testimonial: "I agree with all that Bob MacDonald has said about the putting stroke of Mark G. Harris—and then some."

With his credentials thus established, we may turn to his method and listen respectfully to his views on the subject of which he was the undoubted master. Harris reversed the Bobby Jones dictum that the putt is a miniaturized version of the golf swing. He felt that the putt was the embryo of the golf swing and that each step in the progression from putter to driver was a further magnification of that basic action. It followed, therefore, that conventional teaching was not only hopelessly unbalanced in its concentration on the full swing, and consequent neglect of 50 percent of golf, but was also upside down. Pupils should start with putting and work their way by stages up to the full drive.

Now, this is an unpopular doctrine because novices are naturally anxious to get on with the real thing. Also, many teaching professionals have absorbed and accepted the so-called wisdom of their calling, as enunciated most clearly by the five-time British Open champion J. H. Taylor: "After a fair amount of proficiency has been acquired in the use of the cleek, iron and mashie, we have the difficulty of the putting to surmount. And here I may say at once it is an absolute impossibility to teach a man how to putt." The Harris theory of golf being an extension of putting does at least have the obvious merit of logic, and a measure of proof is available in the chip shot, since this is clearly (or should be) a beefed-up putt played with a more lofted club. In any case, it cannot possibly do any harm to see golf as a progressive magnification of the putt. In practice, it simply means that we must take the proven precepts of good golf and apply them to putting, instead of regarding putting as a game apart with its own rules—or anarchy—of technique. So it follows that, instead of the vast variety of putting styles we see today, we should all aim to acquire a classic putting method and work from there. The tantalizing reward this change of attitude offers is that, if the golfer masters the basic elements of Harris's style of putting, improvements may spread throughout his game:

THE GRIP. It follows naturally from Harris's perception of golf that the putter should be held with the grip to be employed for all shots, that is, the Vardon overlap, with the little finger of the right hand riding on the index finger of the left hand, and with the club held as much in the fingers as possible. Incidentally, Harris's "Boswell," the teacher P. A. Vaile, who meticulously recorded the details of Harris's method for posterity, advanced the iconoclastic theory that one day all golfers would play with the reverse overlap grip, with all the fingers of the right hand on the club and the index finger of the left hand riding over the little finger of the right. Time will tell on that one.

THE STANCE. In accordance with Bobby Jones's insistence on a braced left side for a full shot, Harris put great emphasis on placing the left foot precisely at a right angle to the line of putt, with his weight favoring that foot. Deviations in the placement of the left foot, he felt, either to open or closed positions, tended to cause deviations in the line of the stroke. That square left foot helped to block any tendency for the body to rotate during the stroke and thus push or pull the putt off line.

THE STROKE. Harris rejected both arm-putting and hand-putting. The rocking triangle of arms and shoulders, with the wrists held inflexibly firm, denied the player the benefits of hand action, he felt, and a magnification of that method would be hopeless for full shots. Likewise, restricting the putting action purely to the hands, with the arms held immobilized against the sides, was no basis for golf. The ball must be putted with the genesis of a full swing, that is, with a combination of turn, arm swing, and hand action. Since that movement pivots around a point between the shoulder blades, the shoulders must be bent forward to tilt the pivot in line with the necessary rotation of the shoulders, minute as that might be in the case of a putt. A minute error, however, is enough to make a putt miss the hole. Walter Hagen and Walter Travis, two of the finest putters in the history of professional golf, putted with a pronounced crouch over the ball and stood progressively more erect as they moved up through the bag to longer and longer clubs, which automatically changed the angle of shoulder pivot.

THE PUTT. In moving the club Harris made a miniature swing, in accordance with his principles, and that implies a "release" of the clubhead into the ball as in a full shot rather than a deliberate tap. In practical terms we are probably talking about the same thing, but if we are to make a full commitment to this philosophy of golf it is important to think in the appropriate terminology. Harris even made a distinct rolling, or pronation, of the hands through the impact zone as the Paramount film reveals, and here is the clearest sign in his putting of a full golf shot in its earliest stages of development.

CHIPPING. It is outside the scope of this book to go into chipping, but in the context of the Harris theory it is inevitable because a chip is just a slightly more mature putt. Harris used his mashie (five-iron) for chipping and played it exactly according to the principles outlined above, which remained constant throughout his game.

In effect, Mark G. Harris approached golf like an engineer, positioning his body in the most effective manner to perform a specific function, and simply enlarging that human machine to repeat the function for longer clubs and longer shots.

PITFALLS AMONG THE FINE PRINT

"If the law supposes that," said Mr. Bumble . . . "the law is a ass—a idiot."
—*Charles Dickens*

Once a ball reaches the green a new set of rules comes into play, and so the first thing is to understand what a green is. You already know? You even know the definition? Sure: "All the ground of the hole being played specially prepared for putting."

Sorry, but you are wrong. Every golfer in the world talks about "the green," but technically there is no such thing. The rules of golf specify the *putting* green. Originally, the entire golf course was called the green— hence "green fee," "greenkeepers," and "green committee."

The worthy traditionalists who frame the rules of golf, anxious not to cause confusion in the minds of those who still converse in eighteenth-century English, settled for "putting green," thereby implying that it is an area exclusively used for putting. Such is by no means the case. You may chip or pitch on the putting green if the fancy takes you. There are some holes, like the kidney-shaped seventeenth green at Pebble Beach, for instance, where it is possible for your ball to be on the putting green but for you to find your route to the hole obstructed by an intervening outcrop of rock. Do you have to putt around that rock? Not at all. You are the sole judge of the type of shot you wish to play, and you are perfectly entitled to follow Sam Snead's example and pitch over the rock. If you take a divot out of the sacred turf you may well give the greenkeeper apoplexy, but you will be within your rights.

For the purposes of this chapter we will do what everybody else does and refer simply to the green. So, a ball is on the green if any part of it touches the green. In borderline cases, how can you possibly tell whether the individual blades of grass supporting your ball are growing from the green or from the fringe? Do you send for a referee to make an official ruling on this weighty matter? No, you invoke the most important rule in golf and the only one that is not in the rule book: "If you have to ask, the answer is no."

Golf is constantly producing these fifty-fifty situations in which a millimeter either way may make the difference between playing the ball as it lies or getting a free drop. In such cases the real golfer adjudicates against his own advantage and gets on with the game. In the case above it is a disadvantage to be off the green because you cannot lift and clean the ball or improve the line to the hole, so if there is any doubt in your mind you judge it to be off the green, under the Golden Rule.

One of the bedrock fundamental rules of golf is that you play the ball as it lies. Down the years, golfers with inflated ideas of their own importance, and the importance of their golf, have howled so loudly about their misfortunes that the lawmakers of the game have created more and more exceptions to this admirable principle. A golfer will never fall foul of the law if he plays his ball as it lies, and he will not be troubled by the police if he extends this concept to life itself, and this is the general rule on the green: *you must not touch the line of your putt.* That means, among other things, that you must not step on the line of your putt. Likewise, the rigid courtesies of this honorable game insist that you do not step on the line of anyone else's putt. One of the virtues that sets our game apart from most other sports is that we jealously ensure that the other players have as good a chance as possible of winning.

Nobody will think the worse of you, however, if you avail yourself of the opportunities provided under the rules to give yourself a fair chance with your putt. There are several exceptions to the rule about not touching the line of the putt, and we will take them one by one.

The player may move sand, loose soil, or other loose impediments by picking them up or by brushing them aside with his hand or a club without pressing anything down.

Loose impediments are debris such as stones, leaves, twigs, worms and insects whether dead or alive, casts and heaps made by them, and other natural detritus in addition to sand and loose soil. If you are rash enough to play golf when snow or ice lie on the green, they may be classified as loose impediments and brushed aside or, at your option, you may decree them to be casual water, of which more anon.

The player may remove movable obstructions.

Obstructions are man-made objects and in the context of greens might be cigar butts, nuts and bolts that have fallen off mowing machines, coins previous players have used as ball-markers and left lying around, and—although a remote possibility—champagne corks.

The player may touch the line of his putt in measuring (to determine which ball is farther from the hole), in lifting the ball, and in repairing old hole plugs or ball pitch marks.

The commonest of these procedures is lifting the ball because *whenever a ball is on the green it may be lifted, cleaned if desired, and replaced on its original spot.*

In fact, if you lift your ball properly, as you should, there is no occasion to touch the line of your putt. The approved method of lifting a ball on the green is to approach it along the line of your intended backswing, keeping the ball between you and the hole. You then slide a small coin or similar marker under the back of the ball, if such a term can be applied to a spherical object. At any rate, the marker goes under the ball at the farthest possible point from the hole, which means that throughout this exercise you are well clear of the line of the putt. Now you can lift the ball and clean it if you like. Then, when you are ready to putt, you replace the ball on the *exact* spot from which you lifted it. In replacing the ball, you are perfectly at liberty to line up the maker's name along your target line, and this is a sensible practice as an aid to putting.

There is nothing in the rules to stop you from going through this entire rigamarole of marking, lifting, cleaning, and replacing before you take your second putt as well (or your third, or even—heaven forbid—your fourth). Sometimes such finicky attention to detail is justified, if the green is very sloppy. And it is prudent to mark your ball a second time if you are so mad at missing the first putt that you need a little breathing space to allow your blood pressure to subside before holing out. But many "serious" golfers mark and lift before every putt as a matter of habit, even before tapping in six-inchers. They are entitled to do so under the rules, but those of us whose lives are ebbing away as we have to stand watching their interminable and pointless routines are also entitled to entertain the secret wish that they miss every putt, and every cut, and quietly disappear into well-deserved oblivion.

While we are on the subject of short putts, we might as well deal with the business of tap-ins. On the green the general rule applies that the ball farthest from the hole is played first. So, if you roll a long putt up to the vicinity of the hole, you should, technically, mark it and let the other fellow take his putt. But there is no penalty stroke for playing out of turn, and in the interests of common sense and time-saving when competing at stroke-play you should walk briskly forward and dispatch your ball into the hole, with none of that nonsense about marking and lifting and cleaning. It is true that Harry Vardon once lost a U.S. Open championship by missing a one-inch putt, but that had nothing to do with his failure to lift and clean the ball.

The situation is slightly different in match-play because of the element of psychological warfare. If you hole your tap-in, your opponent is entitled to insist that you replace it and putt in your correct turn, the idea being that the enforced wait will work up such a state of nervous terror that you will miss it when the time comes. In real life, of course, under that Golden Rule for real golfers, as soon as you roll your putt up to six inches your opponent will say words to the effect of "That's good," and thereby concede your next putt.

Every once in a while you will hit what you believe to be a perfect putt, but the ball will stop agonizingly right on the lip, sitting there and peeping over the rim without actually dropping. In that frustrating event you do NOT yell at the top of your voice "Drop, damn you!" You do NOT march to the hole and leap about like a demented dervish in the hope that the vibrations caused by your footfalls will cause the ball to topple into the hole. You do NOT go down on hands and knees and try to blow it over the edge. What you do is this: You walk at an even pace up to the hole and stand there stock still. You wait for ten seconds. If at the end of that period the ball is still above ground, you tap it into the hole. The only problem with this simple routine is that you may not be wearing a watch with a second hand. (Incidentally, it is a sound plan to carry a watch when playing golf because you are allowed only five minutes to search for a lost ball.) So, as your ball sits on the lip insolently defying your desperate attempts to will it into dropping, you can use the trick employed by photographers to time their exposures. You recite in level tones: "One elephant, two elephants, three elephants," and so on. By the time you reach ten elephants, ten seconds will have expired and you must deliver the *coup de grace* with your putter. It is not a bad plan to recite your elephant ritual out loud because, apart from demonstrating your strict adherence to the rules of golf, it may unnerve the opposition.

Back to those exceptions to the rule forbidding you to touch the line of your putt. When the green is soft, the ball is likely to make a dent in the green, known as a pitch mark. Sometimes the ball will actually plop into the green and stay there, sitting in its own pitch mark, or what we call a plugged ball. The rules of golf permit you to repair such damage to the putting surface with no penalty if you touch the line of your putt in doing so. The Golden Rule positively *demands* that you repair pitch marks—and

not just the one made by your ball, but, after you and everyone else in your group has putted out, any others you may find on the green. There are special forks for repairing pitch marks, often supplied free in the pro shop, but carefully applied, a good long tee peg will do the job almost as well. Jab your implement into the turf around the indentation, carefully raising the dent to the original flat surface. Now smooth the area by tapping it *lightly* with the head of your putter. Do not push down as if you were squashing a scorpion; just let the natural weight of the club gently tamp the surface to its pristine state. Experience will tell you where to find your pitch mark. If you have hit a half-top, or caught the ball slightly thin, you are likely to reach the pitch mark before you get to the ball. But if you have really flushed the shot, sending the ball away fizzing with a lovely backspin, your ball may well back up and the pitch mark will be beyond the ball.

Greenkeepers make new holes with a tool that works like an apple-corer. As the greenkeeper withdraws this hole-cutter it removes a plug of turf and soil, which he uses to fill the old hole. It sometimes happens that this plug shrinks and sinks, creating a considerable problem if it happens to be on the line of your putt. You are allowed to repair such damage, but this is often easier said than done. You may be able to lever the old plug out of its hole and make a good job by the judicious use of a handful of sand from a nearby bunker. If your amateur landscaping fails to produce a satisfactory solution, you are entitled to treat the situation as ground under repair, in which case you move your ball to the nearest point that avoids interference by the damaged hole-plug and that is not, of course, nearer the hole.

That exhausts the list of privileges you may employ to make life easier on the green. Now we must move into the area of those stern commandments that demand "Thou shalt not...." The simplest policy here is to remember the Golden Rule and to accept that any action, apart from the exceptions already explained, that might be of the slightest help in making the putt is forbidden. Some of these prohibitions are pretty crazy and would never occur to a real golfer in a million years, but for the sake of thoroughness, we might as well take a look at them.

The yips, or twitch, normally afflict older golfers and can become so severe as to prevent a person from playing the game at all. Indeed, the malady had driven many from the game, when it was discovered that they could obtain an extension of their golfing lives by putting with a croquet action, standing astride the line of the putt and using a long-handled mallet-type putter by swinging it between the legs. It was never a spectacularly successful method, and the only purpose it served was to enable a handful of golfers to continue enjoying a game they had loved, but the lawmakers were appalled at this break with tradition; golf should be played with golf clubs, not with bastardized croquet mallets. So they banned croquet putting. Everybody understands what is meant by croquet putting, for the expression is self-evident, and all that was needed was a simple rule: croquet putting is not allowed. That is how the rules were written back in the year 1774, when the first code of thirteen articles was framed by translating the rules of a French cross-country game and expressing them in simple, direct English which everyone could understand and remember. These days it is obligatory to frame rules in legal jargon comprehensible only by lawyers, so remember this: *The player shall not make a stroke on the putting green from a stance astride, or with either foot touching, the line of the putt or an extension of that line behind the ball. For the purposes of this Clause only, the line of putt does not extend beyond the hole.* (What that second bit means is that if you putt just past the hole, you are allowed to reach across the hole to rake the ball into the hole.)

Once upon a time, the former U.S. and British Open champion, Johnny Miller, was going bananas over his putting. He thought he was swinging along the line of his putt, but in fact he was hitting across the line. In an attempt to save his sanity he had his caddie squat behind him as he putted so that the caddie could report: "You did it again, John. You hit that one across the line." Once again there was consternation in the headquarters of golf at this outbreak of unorthodox behavior. In short order the decree was enacted: *While making a stroke, the player shall not allow his caddie to position himself on or close to an extension of the line of putt behind the ball.* So there you have it. If you have a caddie, you should be sure that he follows the traditional caddie procedure while you are putting, that is, he skulks off to the next tee so that he can steal a cigarette/cigar/swig from the hip flask in your golf bag while your attention is otherwise engaged.

Much more important than all that nonsense is the Golden Rule, which, in this context, requires you to give the other players every chance of making their putts. You stand at the side of the green, well out of their range of vision, keeping silent and still. What you *do not* do is to practice your putting stroke, with or without a ball.

It is not illegal to play a practice stroke after you have putted out, and it is common enough to see a player replay a putt that he has just missed. But it can be a breach of the Golden Rule if it involves wasting time or holding up the players waiting to hit to the green. If you play a practice putt *before* you have putted out, the full weight of the law descends upon you; loss of hole in match-play or two penalty strokes if you are competing at medal or stroke-play.

Such a practice putt is in the same category as the rule that says: *During the play of a hole, a player shall not test the surface of the putting green by rolling a ball or roughening or scraping the surface.* In other words, these are ways in which the player might gain information that would help him with his putt so, therefore, they are *verboten.*

Watch the birdie

The spirit of the Ryder Cup match—Raymond Floyd lands a psychological haymaker on his opponent, 1981.

At a conservative estimate, a golfer takes sixty paces on the green during the process of holing out. By the usual arrangement, each shoe is fitted with eleven metal spikes, or cleats. The traffic for a professional tournament is likely to involve some 130 players, although this figure might easily be doubled on a busy day at a public course. So, by the end of play, every green will have been punctured by about one to two hundred thousand spikes, the concentration being most intense around the hole. Damage from spikes takes three forms: surface holes in which the ball tends to nestle and from which it jumps disconcertingly when contact is made with the putter; raised tuffets, commonly called spike marks, caused by the gouging action of spikes as the foot is lifted; and the scratches and scuffles made by golfers who do not lift their feet clear of the surface in walking or, worse, in turning.

All these forms of damage are aggravating when they occur on your line of putt, as they invariably must and increasingly so as play progresses, and they also represent a source of considerable temptation. It is a sad commentary on human nature, but a matter of simple observation, that many spike marks get repaired under the guise of brushing aside impediments of fixing pitch marks. Thus the European Tour introduced a special tournament rule permitting spike marks to be repaired, and the players naturally fell into the automatic habit of tapping them down. That reflex action had dire consequences at the World Cup of 1980 in Colombia—played under the regular rules of golf, of course—when the French team was disqualified for forgetfully repairing spike marks. A spike mark on the line is just another of those tribulations sent to drive the golfer out of his mind and must be stoically accepted as such—even, as sometimes happens, if you have to take your sand-wedge and chip the ball over a spike mark into the hole.

Among the select company of officials who make up the two rules-of-golf committees, the regulations governing the flag-stick are known as the "Canadian rules." This is because delegates from the Royal Canadian Golf Association were largely instrumental in framing the legislation, a distinction some people feel to be roughly on a par with claiming credit for having invented botulism. After all, what difference would it make to the game of golf if there were no rules *at all* about the flagstick? What if you could take out the flag, or leave it in the hole, as the fancy took you? Would golf suffer? Would putting skill be diminished? Not at all. The only consequence would be that the pace of golf might be fractionally speeded up, and that could only be good. There were no rules in the days when the position of the hole was marked, if at all, by a seagull's feather. Even today it is not obligatory for a club to furnish its course with flagsticks. At Merion, Philadelphia, the sticks are topped by wicker baskets rather than flags, giving the impression that a party of orgiastic Italians has just played the course and rammed a Chianti bottle onto every stick. Such, indeed, may have been the origin of these quaint markers, or something like it, and what could be more appropriate for a fiasco of a game to be ornamented by *fiaschi*? But, if flagsticks are not obligatory, flagstick rules most certainly are, and there is nothing for it but to learn them:

Before and during the stroke, the player may have the flagstick attended, removed, or held up to indicate the position of the hole. This may be done only on the authority of the player before he plays his stroke. Anybody, friend or foe, can implement the player's flagstick instructions, whether these are implied or explicit. The one thing you cannot do is change your mind after you have struck the putt. When the ball is in motion you cannot shout, "Take it out!" or "Put it back!"

So what do you do? Leave the flagstick in the hole? Have it taken out? Have it held up? Or have it attended? These are weighty decisions, and your choice may be influenced by the fact that if your ball hits an unattended flatstick from a stroke played on the green, you are penalized two strokes or loss of hole. So the choice can be narrowed down by resolving never to have the flagstick left in the hole when putting from on the green. If the ball is half an inch off the green, on the fringe, you are quite safe, and should your putt clatter against the flagstick and drop into the hole, you may throw out your chest with pride and reflect that you are a helluva player. Do the same thing when your ball is half an inch on the green and you commit a heinous crime and must be visited by the full rigors of the law, as mentioned above.

Provided that you can see the hole clearly, the sensible and safe policy is to have the flagstick removed. Whoever performs this task should remove it carefully (a careless yank may remove the hole liner along with the flagstick), and take it well away from the player's line of vision, laying it gently on the green, or, better still, on the fringe. With the flagstick out of the way, you can putt with carefree abandon, confident that you are safe from any flagstick penalties.

There are golf courses where the sadistic architect has designed mounds and hollows on the green so severe that as you stand over your putt, you cannot even see the flagstick, let alone the hole. These are the only occasions—and blessedly rare they are too—when there is any justification for having the flagstick held up. (Of course, you will often want the flagstick held up when you are playing an approach shot into a green, and you are entitled to such assistance, but here we are concerned only with putting.)

More commonly, you cannot see the bottom of the flagstick, and you need a point of reference for the aiming of your putt. This is when you ask for the flagstick to be attended, and convention demands that this task be performed in a certain manner. The person attending the flag should stand in such a position that his shadow does not fall across the hole or the line of the putt, with his feet as far from the

hole as is compatible with taking a firm grip on the flagstick, this being to reduce wear and tear in the immediate vicinity of the hole. The flagstick should be held at the top, first gathering the flag into the grip so that it cannot flap and distract the putter. The moment the ball is in motion, the flagstick should be removed from the hole and held well clear so that there is no possibility of its being hit by the ball.

It is not just the flagstick that must not be hit by the ball. The authorized person attending the flagstick is another target to be avoided, under the usual penalties, as well as his equipment. *Equipment?* Yes, indeed. Spare a thought for the feelings of Leonard Thompson putting for an eagle in the Quad Cities Open of 1978. The ball was running sweetly toward the hole, and his caddie, who had dutifully removed the flagstick, was leaping about in excitement at the prospect of a welcome addition to his bonus. A peg tee then fell from behind the caddie's ear and deflected the ball, causing it to miss the hole. With the two-shot penalty, that certain eagle became a bogey.

Golf would be a better game, and the rules could be much simplified, if Rule 1 contained a declaration that golf is an honorable game, played by people who are required to act to the highest levels of sportsmanship, monitoring their own actions at all times and calling appropriate penalties upon themselves when necessary. The penalty for any suspicion of hanky-panky would be disqualification. Essentially, these sentiments define our unofficial Golden Rule, and this is the spirit in which golf has been played for centuries. The legal mind, however, is trained to ignore considerations of morality and ethics, and the rules of golf seek to codify all the game's vast potential for skullduggery and to decree suitable punishments. So the flagstick rules envisage a situation in which your opponent or his caddie might sneakily attend or remove the flagstick without your knowledge or authority. As explained earlier, if you clearly and obviously see him attend the flagstick and make no objection, that counts as giving your authority. So we are discussing a surreptitious act, or possibly a well-intentioned but ignorant act, while you are absorbed in the ritual of lining up your putt. In that case, the opponent loses the hole. Never mind that by snatching the flagstick from the hole he may well have saved you from losing the hole by hitting the stick. That is the law, arguably absurd, probably unnecessary, but sacrosanct. In stroke-play, if a fellow competitor or his caddie attends or removes the flagstick without your authority while you are making your stroke, or after you have struck the ball, he is penalized two strokes. If in these circumstances your ball hits the flagstick or the person attending it, you replay the putt without penalty. If you are playing from off the green, you play the ball as it lies.

The golfer who has absorbed the wisdom and information in the earlier part of this chapter will never putt from on the green to a hole with an unattended flagstick, but, of course, everything changes when putting or chipping from off the green. Then there is no penalty for hitting the flagstick, and it is often sensible—especially when playing downhill—to leave the flagstick in the hole to act as backstop if the ball is traveling too fast. In that case, it frequently happens that the ball lodges against the flagstick without dropping into the hole. *Remember, a ball is holed only when it is at rest within the circumference of the hole and all of it is below the level of the lip of the hole.* When the ball rests against the flagstick it is half in and half out of the hole, and then you (or someone authorized by you) is allowed to move or remove the flagstick. Usually it is enough just to straighten up the flagstick to allow the ball to drop. If so, you have holed out with your last stroke, lucky you. The operation should be performed with care because it is easy enough to move the ball clear of the hole if you snatch out the flagstick. If you wiggle or remove the flagstick and in doing so move the ball without

its dropping into the hole, you must place it on the lip, which is where it probably is already, without penalty. Then you must putt it out in the normal way, reflecting ruefully that a shot of an eighth of an inch counts just as much as a booming drive 280 yards down the fairway.

Many of the regular rules apply equally on the green, of course, with the provision that, in cases through the green where the ball has to be dropped, on the green it must always be *placed*. Probably the most frequently used of these rules is No. 25, covering abnormal ground conditions, of which there are two varieties: casual water *is any temporary accumulation of water which is visible before or after the player takes his stance and is not in a water hazard. Snow and ice are either casual water or loose impediments, at the option of the player. Dew is not casual water.*

At first glance it may seem curious that the rule refers to the water being visible *before or after the player takes his stance.* What that means is that in mushy underfoot conditions, when no water is visible, you must take your normal stance, without excessive stamping of your feet. If you can see water welling up around the soles of your shoes, you are entitled to relief from casual water. But why does the definition also specify water that is visible *before* you take your stance. Surely that is unnecessary since water visible before you take your stance will still be visible after you have taken your stance. The act of taking your stance is not going to make the water disappear, is it? The answer to that question lies within the inscrutable minds of the lawmakers. You might exploit that one the next time you find yourself playing in an important competition on national television. You ball lies in a puddle on the green, and a representative of the committee says, "Hang on a minute, old chap, we'll have the green swept." Men rush out with mechanical devices for removing water, and in a trice the spot where your ball lay is high and dry. But, you do not fancy the putt and inform the referee: "With your

I spy...

There are many ways of capturing that elusive line to the hole—by playing possum like Ian Mosey ...

... by giving it the evil eye, like Isao Aoki ...

... or by sneaking up on it, like Vaughan Somers

...with my little eye

Charlotte Montgomery tries the deep obeisance to the putting god, heedless of the damage spikes can do.

Ken Brown seeks a state of karma through yoga.

While Sandy Lyle blows kisses to the fates.

permission, sir, I propose to take relief under Rule 25-b-111 and *place my ball without penalty in the nearest position to where it lay which affords maximum available relief from the condition, but not nearer the hole nor in a hazard."* The referee will probably point out that since the condition no longer exists, you can hardly take relief from it. That is when you pull out your rule book and demand your rights: "But the water was clearly visible before I took my stance, as you must agree since it was you who ordered it to be mopped up." You may think that such a course of action would breach the spirit of the Golden Rule of sporting behavior, but that is not so. Anything you can do to expose the ludicrously verbose jargon of the rules and thereby persuade the lawmakers to simplify them is not only justified but is your solemn duty.

So, casual water may be soggy ground, puddles, or the overflow above the margins of water hazards. You get free relief if your ball touches such water or if it interferes with your stance or the area of your intended swing. On the green you also get relief if casual water intervenes on the line of your putt. So you place your ball on the nearest spot not nearer the hole that gives you an uninterrupted putting line. Dew, whether visible before or after you take your stance, is a damned nuisance and proof that the green staff has been remiss in its duties, but it is *not* casual water.

Ground under repair is any area so designated by the committee, a hole made by a greenkeeper (but not *the* hole on the green made by a greenkeeper, of course), and material such as grass clippings piled for removal. Technically, holes made by burrowing animals are not ground under repair, but "Certain Damage to Course." The same rules apply, however, so we will lump them altogether under the general heading of "free relief."

The relief procedure described for casual water applies to all these conditions, and so all that remains is to make absolutely sure that we understand what is meant by the various definitions. Material piled for removal, for instance, is a constant source of contention among smart-alec golfers who fancy themselves as barrack-room lawyers. Indeed, it is not unknown for unscrupulous caddies to carry bags of grass clippings and to sprinkle them surreptitiously on a player's ball when it lands in a troublesome spot. In theory, the greenkeeper is the best witness as to whether material has been piled for removal or simply thrown aside to rot, an untidy and prodigal practice since grass clippings should be recycled as compost, thereby saving in expensive fertilizers and reducing the cost of golf. In practice, we must apply common sense.

The location of the pile will provide an important clue and, certainly, if the pile is on a green, it is due for removal. Unless the clippings are fresh it must be assumed that they are not piled for removal. Holes made by a greenkeeper are usually obvious, although there may be confusion over areas from which the greenkeeper has removed turf to resod another part of the course. Are such excavations holes? Ground under disrepair is not necessarily ground under repair, and it is up to the committee to specify the status of such areas. The tricky one is *the hole, cast or runway made by a burrowing animal, a reptile or a bird.* How can you distinguish between the scrape made by a rabbit (which is a burrowing animal under the laws of God and golf) and a dog (which isn't)? And is that circular hole in the turf the mark of a cleat or the hole made by the bill of a bird digging for grubs? Once again, we must fall back on common sense and the Golden Rule. If doubt exists, play the ball as it lies.

Very occasionally a golfer will be faced with a condition of exceptional severity not covered by a rule, like the Walker Cup player whose putt did a U-turn on the green and came back toward him. The reason for this eccentric behavior was that vandals had burned a message on the green with creosote, and the golfer's ball lay in the letter U contained in a well-known expletive usually referred to as Anglo-Saxon, although, in the cause of scholarship, we must insist that it is of Greek origin. If you do run into severe damage so abnormal that it is not covered in the rules, such as vandalism or a gaping crater caused by a meterorite, you may safely treat it as ground under repair and proceed accordingly, making sure to notify the committee when you finish the round and quoting Rule 1-4: *If any point in dispute is not covered by the Rules, the decision shall be made in accordance with equity.*

There is a golf course south of London called Purley Downs with an attractive opening hole, a par-three played steeply downhill to a green nestling in a wooded glade. For most people, the hole calls for an easy five-iron, the perfect way to start a round of golf because it puts no great strain on the player's physical or mental capacities. The hole offers an excellent chance for a par and a pretty good opportunity for a birdie, for most categories of player, and is just the thing to loosen the muscles and put you in a good frame of mind for the coming ordeal. For some years, however, that hole threatened the sanity of half the golf club members and, shame to admit, even drove some of them to strong language and stronger drink.

The reason for this unhappy state of affairs was a fox. This creature lurked in the undergrowth, and when a purely struck golf ball plopped onto the green, the fox ran out, snatched up the ball, and disappeared back into the woods. The local theory was that the fox was the reincarnation of an embittered twenty-four-handicapper because it ignored shots that missed the green. The club was split down the middle into deeply emotional factions about what should be done. One group held that the verminous wretch should be trapped, poisoned, gassed, shot, or summarily dispatched by a combination of all four methods of execution simultaneously. And without further ado. The opposition insisted that not a hair of the fox should be touched. It was, they argued, a delightful natural phenomenon that gave the club a unique and charming distinction. They even had a pet name for it, Freddy.

We will not inquire too deeply into the eventul fate of the fox, and we will ignore malicious rumors about the greenkeeper's wife being seen wearing an overcoat with a very attractive fur collar. The point of the story is that the rules of golf anticipated just such an eventuality. Freddy and his like were already listed as public enemies on two counts, as *outside agencies* and as *burrowing animals.*

We are concerned here with the fox as an outside agency, which is everything—animal, vegetable, or mineral—that is not part of the game. Referees, markers, observers, spectators, other competitors and their golf carts, other golf balls, animals, avalanches, debris blowing about the course, and pretty well anything that might stop, deflect, or remove your ball are outside agencies. Not wind and water, though. The first thing to establish if an outside agency interferes with your ball is whether the ball was at rest or in motion. If the ball was stationary, you replace it without penalty, or, in the case of Freddy, you replace a substitute ball. If a moving ball is stopped or deflected by an outside agency, that is a rub of the green, which is golf talk for "just one of those things," and you play it as it lies, again without penalty.

People who are directly involved in the game, and their equipment, are not outside agencies, obviously enough, and for present purposes we may call them inside agencies, including you, your partner, your opponents, or any of your caddies. Different rules apply to inside agencies, and we deal first with those occasions when the ball is at rest.

If you or your partner or your caddies illegally moves or touches your ball on purpose, you are penalized one stroke and the ball must be replaced. There is no penalty *on the green* if the ball moves while you are clearing away loose impediments, but

Hey Toro!

If you come from Spain, like Seve Balles-teros, the adversary has horns and you naturally act accordingly.

A leap for safety

elsewhere on the course this too costs a penalty stroke. In match-play, if your opponent or his caddie touches or moves your ball illegally, he is penalized one stroke. If you or your caddie moves your ball illegally, you are penalized one stroke. This sort of accident is not so uncommon as you might think: Roger Wethered lost the British Amateur Championship against Bobby Jones because, as he walked backward alongside the line of his putt intently calculating how much it might break, he kicked the ball with his heel. In stroke-play, if a fellow competitor or his caddie accidentally moves your ball, there is no penalty and the ball is replaced. There is one important exception to that rule. Suppose your group plays to a green and a fellow competitor carelessly mistakes your ball for his and putts it? Well, he does not count that putt as a stroke, but he *does* get a two-stroke penalty, and he must then putt out with his own ball. Your ball must be replaced. If your opponent did this in match-play, he would lose the hole.

The rules for stopping or deflecting a moving ball follow the same logic, designed to produce a fair solution to an unfortunate incident. Thus if your side is the culprit, you lose the hole in match-play. If

An elegant passe

And coup de grace

the opposition is responsible there is no penalty, provided the interference was accidental. You can either play the ball as it lies or replay the stroke. But if the opposition *deliberately* stops or deflects your ball, that player loses the hole and may be disqualified.

In stroke-play, if your side stops or deflects your ball, you are penalized two strokes and the ball is played as it lies. Your fellow competitiors and their caddies are outside agencies, so in cases of accidental interference there are no penalties and you play the ball as it lies. But if your ball should be stopped or deflected by a fellow competitor deliberately—perish the thought —the culprit should be dragged to the nearest tree and hanged, drawn, and quartered. Actually, the rules of golf merely specify disqualification in such cases because neither the United States Golf Association nor the Royal and Ancient Golf Club of St. Andrews has the authority to impose capital punishment, more's the pity.

If your ball is on the green and you putt and it hits a stationary ball which is also on the green, in stroke-play you are penalized two strokes—and it serves you right because there is no possible excuse for such folly in that you are entitled to have other balls lifted at any time, and should always do so if there is the slightest danger of hitting them.

There is one situation in which you can touch your ball on the green and see it move with impunity, and that is in addressing it for a putt. But we must be absolutely clear about the rights and wrongs of such incidents. It often happens that when a player grounds his putter behind the ball— or even in front of it if he happens to be one of those strange characters who thinks that this ritual helps—the weight of the clubhead on the turf causes the ball to roll against the face of the putter. As soon as the player relieves the pressure on the turf by fractionally raising the putter, the ball rocks back into its original position. Such movement is perfectly allowable, provided that the ball really does rock back into its

original position. But if the ball moves, then stays in a different position when the putter is grounded, you must call a penalty stroke on yourself. Generally, you are the only person who knows whether the ball has moved position, and it should not be a matter for self-congratulation when you call the penalty stroke on yourself, nor for congratulation by others. Whether the ball has moved position is a matter of *fact,* and, if it has, the penalty is the automatic reaction. The whole process should be as natural as accidentally swallowing a fly, a nuisance and not exactly pleasant but hardly worthy of comment one way or another.

If any golfer has the slightest doubt about his ability to ignore those internal demons who suggest, "Go on, ignore it, nobody else saw it move," there is a simple solution. All he has to do is get into the habit of never grounding his club on the green. Likewise, it is always wise to refrain from grounding your club in the rough. That way, if your ball should move after you have taken your stance, it is none of your doing and there is no question of penalty.

You might imagine that the list of do's and don'ts on the green must be exhausted by now, but there are a few other ways in which a golfer can fall foul of the rules on the green. There is the actual stroke, about which the law says: *The ball shall be fairly struck at with the head of the club and must not be pushed, scraped or spooned.* The green is the most likely place for such an infringement to occur, especially with those tiny little putts that often have to be played when the golfer is in a heightened emotional state. Do not lean forward and drag the ball into the hole because that could be interpreted as scraping. Dispatch such putts with a firm tap. Nerves are a factor on the greens, more so than elsewhere, and when a player is handling his putter as if it were a live snake it is easy enough to make the sort of tentative jab at the ball that results in striking it twice. To add injury to indignity, that has to go down on the card as two strokes.

This great body of legislation may sound very complicated, but in reality it is simple enough for adherents to the Golden Rule. If you behave honorably, and with due sportsmanship and consideration for others on the green, keeping within the law boils down to doing what comes naturally.

We have now covered the basics of putting law, the bare bones of formal legislation. There is more, much more, however, because a vital part of the glorious lunacy of the game of golf is the freakish incident for which the rules do not, on the face of it, provide a ready solution. Actually, it is nearly always possible to find the correct solution, even if that means submitting the conundrum to the Rules of Golf Committee for expert interpretation. That is not possible at the time, of course, so you apply the Golden Rule, and for once the law is on your side, providing as it does (Rule 1) for you to make a decision in accordance with equity. The answers to formal queries are published as decisions, and they often provide a valuable insight into the intention behind a rule as well, in some cases, as a little harmless entertainment.

For instance, perhaps once in your lifetime you will hit a perfect approach shot and the ball will plug in the side of the hole. Have you holed out? If all of the ball is below ground level the answer is yes, even though it is not within the circumference of the hole as required by the definition. But if part of the ball is above the lip, you can either play it or lift it, repair the damage under the plugged-ball rule, replace the ball, and putt it.

There are puddles on the line of your putt. Can you sweep the water aside or mop it up with a towel? No. Casual water is not a loose impediment. What you can do is to move your ball to the nearest point not nearer the hole that gives you an uninterrupted putting line to the hole.

The green is liberally carpeted with leaves fallen from an overhanging tree. To save time, you clear the line of your putt by flapping vigorously with your cap. Is that permitted? No. You may use only your hand or club to brush aside loose impediments.

In a match you ask your opponent to attend the flagstick, and, as he gets near the hole, he deliberately steps on your line and grinds his heel into the turf, guaranteeing that your putt will be deflected. What is the correct procedure? He loses the hole. If a committee member sees the incident, your opponent should be disqualified. It is entirely up to you if, later, in the privacy of the locker room, you punch him in the mouth. In any case, never play golf with him again and see to it that he is expelled from your club.

In the same vein, you are playing a medal competition and a fellow competitor holes a huge putt. His caddie, who is attending the flag, jumps up and down in ecstasy and makes a deep footprint slap bang on your line. Can you repair the damage before you putt? No. Footprints are not among the conditions you are allowed to fix. You can ask the committee to repair the damage if there is an official at hand. You would be entirely in order in asking your fellow competitor to make his caddie behave properly in the future.

Can you hold the flagstick in one hand and tap in your short putt one-handed with the other? Yes. You can also hold your umbrella over you and putt one-handed, but you cannot have your caddie hold the umbrella to shield you from the elements while you putt.

Now, here is everyone's absolute favorite golf decision. Is a snake an outside agency? Well, the answer is that a dead snake is a loose impediment, but that decision obviously raises another vital question: How do you know for sure whether a snake is alive or dead? There is a nicely established convention that a golfer is not required to put himself into physical danger, and this can be very important in places where the wildlife is unfriendly. In Africa, for example, no sensible person goes near a swarm of wild bees or a grazing rhino.

The Rules of Golf Committee was once asked to adjudicate in a dispute between two women golfers who were playing a

The dance of delight

The Turkey Trot by an elated Fuzzy Zoeller.

A Funky Chicken as Sandra Post celebrates.

match when one of them hit an approach shot into a bunker, the ball coming to rest next to a coiled rattlesnake. The woman asked her opponent if she had to play the ball as it lay. Women take their golf tremendously seriously, and the opponent answered that certainly she had to play the ball as it lay, adding helpfully that she herself would stand by with a rake at the ready to deter the snake if it tried to strike. What if the snake struck first? Do not worry, my dear, in that case you may rest assured that due retribution shall be delivered upon the evil serpent that took your life and cost you the match. The Rules of Golf Committee eventually pondered this issue and in due season handed down a judgment: the player should have been permitted to drop another ball in a similar bunker, roughly equidistant from the hole and in a comparable lie.

So there we have a valuable precedent to guide our actions when confronted with creatures of the wild. On the specific question of determining whether a snake should be treated as an outside agency or a loose impediment, the best advice is to announce firmly to your opponent: "Although it is not moving, I deem that snake to be asleep. I further deem it to be extremely

Mark James and a solo Highland Fling.

The chorus, Eamon Darcy and Bernard Gallacher.

bad-tempered and highly dangerous, and therefore I propose to drop another ball in a similar but distant position. If you disagree with that proposal I am willing to withdraw to a safe place while you advance and prod the brute with your wedge. If it proves to be a loose impediment, then I authorize you to remove it and fling it into those bushes, in which case I will play my ball as it lies."

At a short hole you hit your tee shot close to the flagstick. As you are walking forward a gust of wind blows the ball into the hole. What is the position? You have holed in one. Congratulations. Wind is not an outside agency. Now, say that you have played a similar shot, but this time you walk forward and mark your ball. When you replace your ball, but before you address it, the wind blows it into the hole. Obviously you have played one stroke and taken the ball out of play before the hole is completed. What is your procedure? The same. You still have to buy drinks all round in the bar afterward because the wind is *still* not an outside agency. There is no provision in the rules, therefore, for you to replace the ball. You are deemed to have holed out with your previous stroke (rather an unsatisfactory decision because it defies logic, but that is the way the wind blows).

You hit an approach shot, but from where you stand, part of the green and all the adjoining area of fairway, bunker, and dry water hazard are obscured from your view. As you approach, you see a boy running away with a ball in his hand. The boy drops the ball, and you identify it as yours. What do you do next? Since it is clear that the boy picked up your ball, but you cannot judge where it may have been lying, you must resort to equity. You therefore drop the ball in a place that is neither the most favorable nor the least favorable to you. In other words, you do a rough assessment of the degree of difficulty of the possible lie in that area and choose a spot that registers as a five on the scale of ten.

A cloudburst drenches the course just as you play into a green. As you walk forward you see a rivulet of casual water sweep your ball off the green into a bunker. Knowing that the rules seek to be fair at all times, you imagine that, in equity, you must be entitled to redress such a miscarriage of justice and replace your ball on the putting surface. Is that correct? No, it is not. Water is not an outside agency, so you have to accept your misfortune and play the ball from where it now lies in the bunker.

We have already discussed the need for the person attending a flagstick to exercise care in removing it because of the danger of wrenching out the hole liner. Suppose that happens and the liner is lifted clear of the hole and your ball drops into the unlined hole. Was that putt legitimate? Yes, it was. The putt was good, and there is no penalty. Suppose the liner came halfway out of the hole and stuck there with its rim above the level of the putting surface. What is the position if your ball now hits the liner? This time the rule of equity comes to your aid and you play the ball as it lies, without penalty.

We all concede short putts to opponents. In the case of tiddlers for which the tapping in is a mere formality, such concessions are part of a long and honorable tradition, a simple act of courtesy that should be acknowledged as such. Some people, however, get the idea that they have a right to have every putt under three feet or so conceded and that failure to concede is a breach of sportsmanship. That attitude is nonsensical. There is no obligation, moral or legal, to concede a putt, and if there is the slightest chance that your opponent might miss one, even of only twelve inches, you owe yourself a duty to see the ball safely dispatched into the hole. It is unwise to *expect* a concession, and quite out of order to suggest, overtly or by oblique hints, that a sporting gesture would not go amiss. Always expect and be prepared to hole out even the shortest of putts, and then you will not be upset if no concession is offered. And, most important, make absolutely sure when you are conceding a putt that your meaning is clear.

For instance, the common expression, "That's good," could be used to convey congratulations for a skillful approach putt, but it could equally be interpreted as a concession of the next putt. Severiano Ballesteros is fond of telling of his experience at the World Match-play Championship when he made just such a complimentary remark about a long approach putt that finished three feet from the hole. His opponent said, "Thank you," picked up his ball, and walked to the next tee. The galling part of that story is that the opponent was one Arnold Palmer!

Now for a few legal tangles that can arise from concessions. You putt up close to the hole with your third stroke and your opponent concedes the tiddler. Then, in attempting to knock your ball back to you, he inadvertently hits it into the hole. You claim to be down in three. Is that correct? No. He conceded your fourth stroke, and at that point you had completed the hole. What happened after the concession is irrelevant.

You hit your tee shot at a blind par-three, then, when you reach the green, your ball is nowhere to be seen. You search for five minutes in vain and then concede the hole. Your opponent says he will putt out anyway, just for the hell of it, and in doing so he finds your ball in the hole. Who wins the hole? You do—and you also buy the drinks because you have holed in one. Nothing can change the fact that your first shot went into the hole, and conceding the hole in ignorance of the fact does not change the fact.

Here is a sad little cautionary tale about concessions. You hole out, and, thinking you have won the match, pick up your opponent's ball and shake him warmly by the hand. Your warmth is not reciprocated by your opponent, who tells you in no uncertain terms that the match is not over. He had that putt to win the hole and keep the match alive. You are forced, on due reflection, to agree that such is indeed the case. The question now arises as to whether the act of picking up your opponent's ball constituted a concession of his next putt. What do you think? Bad luck. You are penalized a stroke for touching an opponent's ball, and he must replace it.

Your opponent's ball is on the line of your putt and you ask him to mark it. Instead, he taps his ball into the hole. Can you claim the hole on the grounds that he failed to comply with a rule of golf? No, but you can require him to replay the putt in the correct order of play.

Here is a real beauty that should be taken on appeal to the United Nations Committee on Human Rights. You mark and lift your ball on the green and toss it to your caddie to be cleaned. The caddie misses his catch, and the ball falls into a lake and cannot be retrieved. You take the only course of action open to you, taking out a new ball from your bag and putting out with it. Is that correct? Indeed, it is not. In match-play you lose the hole for playing a wrong ball. In stroke-play you are liable for disqualification, although the Rules of Golf Committee in its infinite charity recommends that the committee commute your sentence to a penalty of two strokes. You may think this judgment to be excessively harsh. Surely a stroke and distance penalty in the spirit of the lost-ball regulations would be more suitable, you may feel. Well, you are perfectly entitled to think that the ruling is ludicrous, but there it is; that is the law.

Of course, this is a rather farfetched case that happens only once in a blue moon, but there are other and much more likely ways in which you can inadvertently substitute a wrong ball on the green. For instance, plenty of golfers carry a spare ball in the pocket, ready to be used as a provisional ball and getting warmed up to body heat in the process, a useful precaution in cold weather because a warm ball goes farther. In that case, it is all too easy to lift a ball on the green, pop it into your pocket, and then accidentally replace the wrong one. If you discover the error before hitting your tee shot on the next hole, you have an opportunity to salvage something from the wreckage by replaying that putt, or putts, with the correct ball and taking a penalty of two strokes. Putts played with the wrong ball are not counted. You could not follow this procedure in the case of the ball falling into the lake because the correct ball could not be retrieved. If you discover your mistake *after* hitting a shot on the next tee, you are disqualified.

An incident during the World Match-play Championship illustrates the importance of establishing the facts, and *all* the facts, before attempting to decide a ruling. Nick Faldo and Graham Marsh were playing a match, and they—and the referee—had their sight of the green obscured by trees when Faldo hit an approach shot that pitched on the back of the green and hopped over it. When the players and officials arrived at the green, a marshal informed the referee that Faldo's ball had been deflected by a spectator. The referee asked if the ball was in motion at the time. Upon being assured that such was the case, the referee ordered that Faldo must play his ball as it lay. It lay nicely on the green, in fact, because it had been deliberately kicked back by a partisan spectator. Faldo was subjected to considerable abuse because he did not offer Marsh a half or concede his putt. Actually, not having witnessed the incident, Faldo was blameless. All he did was play to the instructions of the referee. The fault lay with the marshal for not reporting the full facts. If he had told the referee that there had been deliberate interference, the official would have been in a position to make the correct decision, which would have been for Faldo to drop his ball at the place where it was kicked.

APPENDIX

Below are the formal legalities covering putting from the *Rules of Golf:*

Rule 16. The Putting Green

Definitions
The "putting green" is all ground of the hole being played which is specially prepared for putting or otherwise defined as such by the Committee. A ball is on the putting green when any part of it touches the putting green.

A ball is "holed" when it is at rest within the circumference of the hole and all of it is below the level of the lip of the hole.

16-1. General
a. Touching Line of Putt
The line of putt must not be touched except:
  (i) the player may move sand, loose soil and other loose impediments by picking them up or by brushing them aside with his hand or a club without pressing anything down;
 (ii) in addressing the ball, the player may place the club in front of the ball without pressing anything down;
(iii) in measuring—Rule 10–4;
 (iv) in lifting the ball—Rule 16–1b;
  (v) in repairing old hole plugs or ball marks—Rule 16–1c; and
 (vi) in removing movable obstructions—Rule 24–1.
(Indicating line for putting on putting green—Rule 8–2b.)

b. Lifting Ball
A ball on the <u>putting green</u> may be lifted and, if desired, cleaned. A ball so lifted shall be replaced on the spot from which it was lifted.

c. Repair of Hole Plugs and Ball Marks
The player may repair an old hole plug or damage to the <u>putting green</u> caused by the impact of a ball, whether or not the player's ball lies on the putting green. If the ball is moved in the process of such repair, it shall be replaced, without penalty.

d. Testing Surface
During the play of a hole, a player shall not test the surface of the <u>putting green</u> by rolling a ball or roughening or scraping the surface.

e. Standing Astride or on Line of Putt
The player shall not make a <u>stroke</u> on the <u>putting green</u> from a <u>stance</u> astride, or with either foot touching, the line of the putt or an extension of that line behind the ball. For the purpose of this Clause only, the line of putt does not extend beyond the hole.

f. Position of Caddie or Partner

While making the <u>stroke,</u> the player shall not allow his caddie, his partner or his partner's caddie to position himself on or close to an extension of the line of putt behind the ball.

g. Other Ball to Be at Rest

A player shall not play a stroke or touch his ball in play while another ball is in motion after a stroke on the putting green.

h. Ball Overhanging Hole

When any part of the ball overhangs the edge of the hole, the player is allowed enough time to reach the hole without unreasonable delay and an additional ten seconds to determine whether the ball is at rest. If by then the ball has not fallen into the hole, it is deemed to be at rest.

PENALTY FOR BREACH OF RULE 16–1:
Match play—Loss of hole; Stroke play—Two strokes.

16-2. Conceding Opponent's Next Stroke

When the opponent's ball is at rest or is deemed to be at rest, the player may concede the opponent to have holed out with his next stroke and the ball may be removed by either side with a club or otherwise.

Rule 17.   The Flagstick

17–1.   Flagstick Attended, Removed or Held Up

Before and during the <u>stroke</u> the player may have the flagstick attended, removed or held up to indicate the position of the hole. This may be done only on the authority of the player before he plays his stroke.

If the flagstick is attended or removed by an opponent, a fellow-competitor or the caddie of either with the player's knowledge and no objection is made, the player shall be deemed to have authorized it. If a player or a caddie attends or removes the flagstick or stands near the hole while a stroke is being played, he shall be deemed to attend the flagstick until the ball comes to rest.

If the flagstick is not attended before the stroke is played, it shall not be attended or removed while the ball is in motion.

17–2.   Unauthorized Attendance

a. Match Play

In match play, an opponent or his caddie shall not attend or remove the flagstick without the player's knowledge or authority.

b. Stroke Play

In stroke play, if a fellow-competitor or his caddie attends or removes the flagstick without the competitor's knowledge or authority while the competitor is making a stroke or his ball is in motion, *the fellow-competitor shall incur the penalty* for breach of this Rule. In such circumstances, if the competitor's ball strikes the flagstick or the person attending it, the competitor incurs no penalty and the ball shall be played as it lies, except that, if the stroke was played from the putting green, the stroke shall be replayed.

Match play—Loss of hole; Stroke play—Two strokes.

17–3.   Ball Striking Flagstick or Attendant

The player's ball shall not strike:

a. The flagstick when attended or removed by the player, his partner or either of their caddies, or by another person with the player's knowledge or authority; or

b. The player's caddie, his partner or his partner's caddie when attending the flagstick, or another person attending the flagstick with the player's knowledge or authority, or <u>equipment</u> carried by any such person; or

c. The flagstick in the hole, unattended, when the ball has been played from the <u>putting green.</u>

PENALTY FOR BREACH OF RULE 17–3:
Match play—Loss of hole; Stroke play—Two strokes, and the ball shall be played as it lies.

17–4. Ball Resting Against Flagstick

If the ball rests against the flagstick when it is in the hole, the player or someone authorized by him may move or remove the flagstick and if the ball falls into the hole, the player shall be deemed to have holed out at his last stroke; otherwise the ball, if <u>moved,</u> shall be placed on the lip of the hole, without penalty.

BIBLIOGRAPHY

Ballesteros, Severiano, and Dudley Doust. *Seve: The Young Champion.* London: Hodder and Stoughton, 1982.

Bolt, Tommy. *How to Keep Your Temper on the Golf Course.* New York: David McKay, 1969.

Browning, Robert. *History of Golf: The Royal and Ancient Game.* New York: Dutton, 1955.

Casper, Billy. *My Million Dollar Shots.* New York: Grosset and Dunlap, 1970.

Cornish, Geoffrey, and Ronald Whitten. *The Golf Course.* New York: Rutledge Press, 1981.

Devlin, Bruce. *Play Like the Devil.* Sydney: Angus and Robertson, 1967.

Gallwey, Timothy. *The Inner Game of Golf.* New York: Random House, 1979.

Golf Digest. *All About Putting.* New York: Coward McCann, 1973.

Lema, Tony. *Champagne Golf.* New York: McGraw Hill, 1966.

Mackenzie, Dr. Alister. *Dr. Mackenzie's Golf Architecture.* Droitwich: Grant, 1982.

Michael, Tom. *Golf's Winning Stroke.* New York: Coward McCann, 1967.

Park, Willie, Jr. *The Art of Putting.* London: Gray, 1920.

Player, Gary. *Golf's Secrets.* New York: Prentice-Hall, 1962.

Price, Charles. *The World of Golf.* New York: Random House, 1962.

Rees, Dai. *Golf My Way.* London: Heinemann, 1951.

Snead, Sam. *Golf Begins at Forty.* New York: Doubleday, 1979.

The Handbook of Putting. London: Pelham, 1975.

United States Golf Association and the Royal and Ancient Golf Club of St. Andrews. *The Rules and Decisions of Golf,* 1984.

Vaile, P. A. *Putting Made Easy.* Chicago: Reilly and Lee, 1935.

Watson, Tom, and Nick Seitz. *Getting Up and Down.* New York: Random House, 1983.

Williams, David. *The Science of the Golf Swing.* London: Pelham, 1969.

Young Douglas. *St. Andrews—Town and Gown, Royal and Ancient.* London: Cassell, 1969.

Picture Credits

DRAWINGS   Courtesy of Chris Perfect

BLACK-AND-WHITE PHOTOGRAPHS 2, 8, 12, 13, 18, 19, 24, 52, 79, 94, 98, 99, 136, 142, 146, 147, 150, 151, 154, 155: courtesy of Phil Sheldon; 96, 103 (top): courtesy of The Press Association Ltd.; 100, 101, 102 (bottom three), 104, 105: courtesy of AP Wirephotos; 102 (top three): courtesy of Associated Sports Photography; 103 (bottom): courtesy of Wide World Sports.

COLOR PHOTOGRAPHS 29, 40, 43: courtesy of Lawrence N. Levy; 32, 38, 44, 46, 48: courtesy of Phil Sheldon.

ARNOLD PALMER is one of golf's all-time superstars. His charging style of play and his charismatic personality did much to bring about the tremendous growth in the popularity of golf during the 1960s. The winner of seven major championships and sixty-one PGA Tour titles, Palmer now competes regularly on the Senior Tour, and is credited for much of its spectacular success. He lives with his wife, Winnie, in Latrobe, Pennsylvania, and Orlando, Florida.

PETER DOBEREINER is recognized world-wide as one of the most knowledgeable, entertaining, and colorful writers on the game of golf. The author of many books, and a regular contributor to *Golf Digest* magazine, Dobereiner lives with his wife, Betty, in a rambling old house in Kent, England.